Dewey for Artists

Dewey for Artists

Mary Jane Jacob

The University of Chicago Press

Chicago and London

The University of Chicago Press, Chicago 60637
The University of Chicago Press, Ltd., London
© 2018 by The University of Chicago
Published 2018

27 26 25 24 23 22 21 20 19 18   1 2 3 4 5

ISBN-13: 978-0-226-58030-2 (cloth)
ISBN-13: 978-0-226-58044-9 (paper)
ISBN-13: 978-0-226-58058-6 (e-book)
DOI: https://doi.org/10.7208/chicago/9780226580586.001.0001

Library of Congress Cataloging-in-Publication Data
Names: Jacob, Mary Jane, author.
Title: Dewey for artists / Mary Jane Jacob.
Description: Chicago ; London : The University of Chicago Press, 2018. |
Includes bibliographical references and index.
Identifiers: LCCN 2018028791 | ISBN 9780226580302 (cloth : alk. paper) |
ISBN 9780226580449 (pbk. : alk. paper) | ISBN 9780226580586 (e-book)
Subjects: LCSH: Dewey, John, 1859–1952. | Art—Philosophy.
Classification: LCC B945.D44 J336 2018 | DDC 191—dc23
LC record available at https://lccn.loc.gov/2018028791

Contents

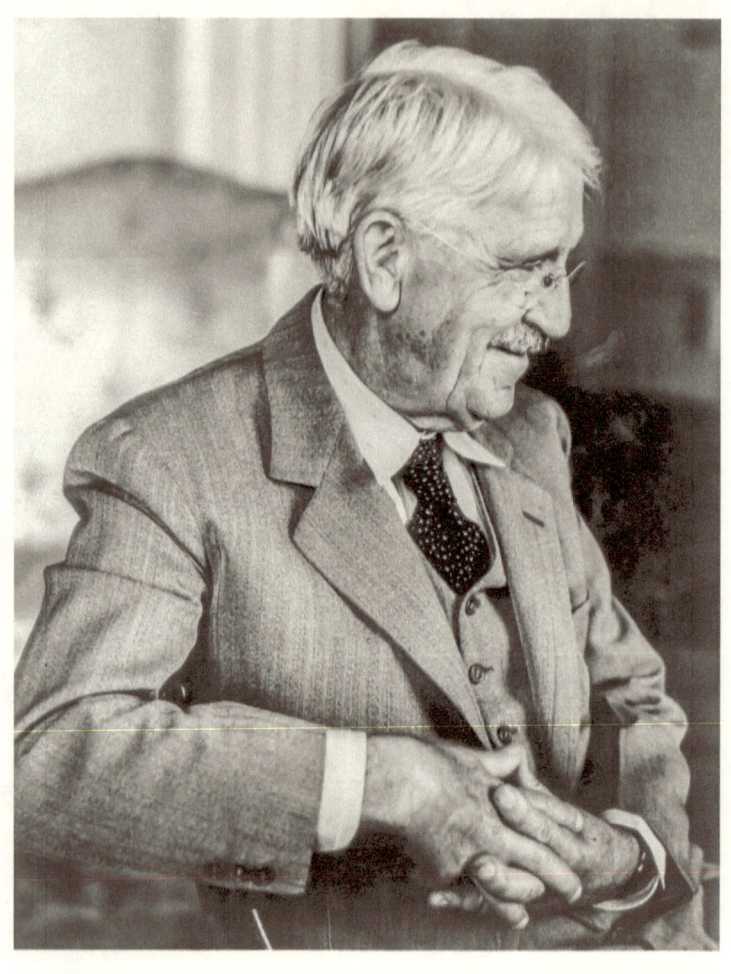

Portrait of John Dewey, n.d. Special Collections Research Center, Morris Library, Southern Illinois University, Carbondale. Photo: Sylvia Salmi.

Introduction

We come to John Dewey through American culture, through the lives we live and the institutions we protect—and whose erosion we bemoan, like he did, saying democracy is gone, co-opted, hopelessly compromised, if it ever did exist.[1] We also find in Dewey a steadfast believer in art, not art as a subject or objects, but as a way of being in the world. Dewey is one of those authors whose vast writings have occasioned equally vast literature. His works are assembled in thirty-seven volumes—early, middle, and later works—and his correspondence and class lectures have been compiled. Thus, this book could have been a daunting or, worse yet, a redundant enterprise.

In recent years I have read Dewey for my own purposes, but it was only after I got past *Art as Experience* and read him more broadly that I found his resolve and relevance all the greater. I lived through the Culture Wars of the late 1980s, when the National Endowment for the Arts (NEA) became a battleground where artists were vilified as amoral and art deemed a wasteful use of taxpayer dollars. But to Dewey, artists were foundational in envisioning and creating a democratic society, even as some sectors of American society have always been suspect of art's value. So while his name was seldom invoked in that era, the Conservative campaign—then as now—sought to dismantle the groundwork he had laid and the values for which he stood. Organizations formed in art's defense and foundations bolstered the NEA's funds, which were dwindling especially for individual artists. In further retaliation, social practice art, which took politicized forms in the seventies and eighties, rose with heightened fury in the nineties. But Reaganomics' trend toward privatization won out, making the art market all the stronger and our social problems all the deeper.

For my part, I fled the marketing-oriented, donor-obligated arena of the art museum, landing in the contested public space of the city where I gravitated to art whose controversial content aligned with publics whose visibility and agency were — well, in Deweyan terms — eclipsed. I sought to find out: Was there still potential for the kind of transformative aesthetic experience that was so central to Dewey's understanding of life? And could we be open not only to our own experiences but to those of others? In this, I was spurred on by Dewey, who knew from his own life experiences that when we truly experience art, we absorb it and are changed.

Still I wondered why Dewey's philosophy had fallen out of favor when artists as diverse as Marcel Duchamp, Josef Albers, Robert Motherwell, and Allan Kaprow all read *Art as Experience*. Had Dewey's view of what art is become skewed by means of the paperback edition that art students are required to read but from which the philosopher's carefully chosen illustrations are removed? They tell a wider story: *The Winged Victory*, Pueblo Indian pottery, Bushman rock-painting, a Scythian ornament, El Greco's *Gethsemane*, Renoir's *Bathers*, a Cezanne *Still Life*, a work of "Negro Sculpture," and Matisse's *Joie de Vivre*. Or perhaps Dewey's taste in art was too populist, just too middlebrow, his sweeping view of art not elitist and avant-garde enough? Maybe his understanding of a human community sounded too universalist in an era of postcolonial discourse and identity politics? Or did he just slip from memory in an art world that is continually reinventing itself, casting a shadow over earlier histories, subverting their legacies?

Then there is Dewey's politics. Was he just too American in his outlook for a younger power-to-the-people generation for whom anti-Americanism was a rallying point in the 1960s, or for a later globally minded one? It is true that for all his gripes about capitalism, Dewey never gave up on democracy and the possibility for a humane way of life in the United States that could serve as a beacon in the world. He put the social concerns of his times directly into his life and work — never leaving art on the sidelines — as he fought for workers' rights and called for greater social responsibility in the late 1920s, showed the way through the hard times of the 1930s, illuminated the role of the United States on the international scene in the 1940s, and took up causes till the very end, championing as he was defining American Liberalism, giving substance to what it is to be a Progressive.

Already by the 1950s, McCarthyism had begun expunging him from public consciousness, seeing his liberal social reforms as communist, for surely Dewey would have been on the rack had he lived another year, with his decades-long record of political actions and his faith in the capacity of human beings rather than in God. Even the field of public education, in which he had been consistently read and beloved by many, could not keep him in the public forefront. By the fifties, his views on Progressive education made him a pariah in the classroom, and what residue remains today in the US public school system is repeatedly prone to cuts.

As attention moved to Marxist and Postmodern theorists and the Frankfurt School, Dewey was left behind. Perhaps an explanation for why he is not a favored art theorist may be, quite simply, because he never divided theory from practice. To look for that in Dewey is to misunderstand the very nature of experience, to which he was dedicated. So I will not be doing a service to philosophers and theorists, before and after Dewey, by citing influences and followers. I will depend on Dewey for Dewey.

His presence spanned half the nineteenth century and half the twentieth, and connections can be made both backward and forward. Dewey was born in 1859, the year Darwin's *Origin of the Species* was first published and two short years before the start of the Civil War. At a young age, he felt the country come apart, then put itself back together and become more powerful than any modern nation. Dewey was among those who reminded us of the founding principles and tried to make them real. Even at the advanced age of eighty, he was writing to give immediate relevance to the thoughts of Thomas Jefferson.[2]

Dewey and I share the terrain of Chicago: the midwestern city of his compatriot Jane Addams, a place rife with class conflict and social deprivation, where Dewey found a training ground and had his conversion.[3] Yet the formative geographical locus for me was not Chicago but Charleston, South Carolina, when I was invited to curate a show. This location opened me up to a world in which life is understood as experience lived not just in a lifetime but over centuries and embodied by successive generations. The resulting exhibition, *Places with a Past*, looked at America's history through temporary installations sited around this former port of entry for slaves from West Africa, but the artists' works were more than smart, postcolonial critiques. Through their sited-ness and their publics (the families that have lived there) they came alive — so much so that long after the exhibition's close, after the material existence of most works ended, the experience of them continued to unfold among artists, curators, visitors, funders, institutions, catalog readers and lecture audiences, and not least of all Charleston residents. Ten years later, a chance came to return for another project, but in the end it was not one but a series of unfolding, discursive, and artistic actions. Over a decade, a strong, continuous thread of meaning was woven that came to be known as *Places with a Future*.[4]

In the early nineties, I also engaged Chicago with *Culture in Action*,[5] an experimental exhibition as social intervention that took root in different communities, among diverse constituencies around the city. At its heart lay questions around what art can mean in the everyday: Can it address the critical concerns of people who do not identify with the art world or go to museums? Can art's processes be lived by those involved in an artist's project? The debates this exhibition spawned in the art world — on what constitutes a work of art, its authorship, and audiences — were played out a couple years later in *Conversations at the Castle: Changing Audiences and Contemporary Art*.[6] For this counter-Olympic program based in a derelict nineteenth-century mansion ("the Castle"), artists from other parts of the world came to Atlanta. Half of

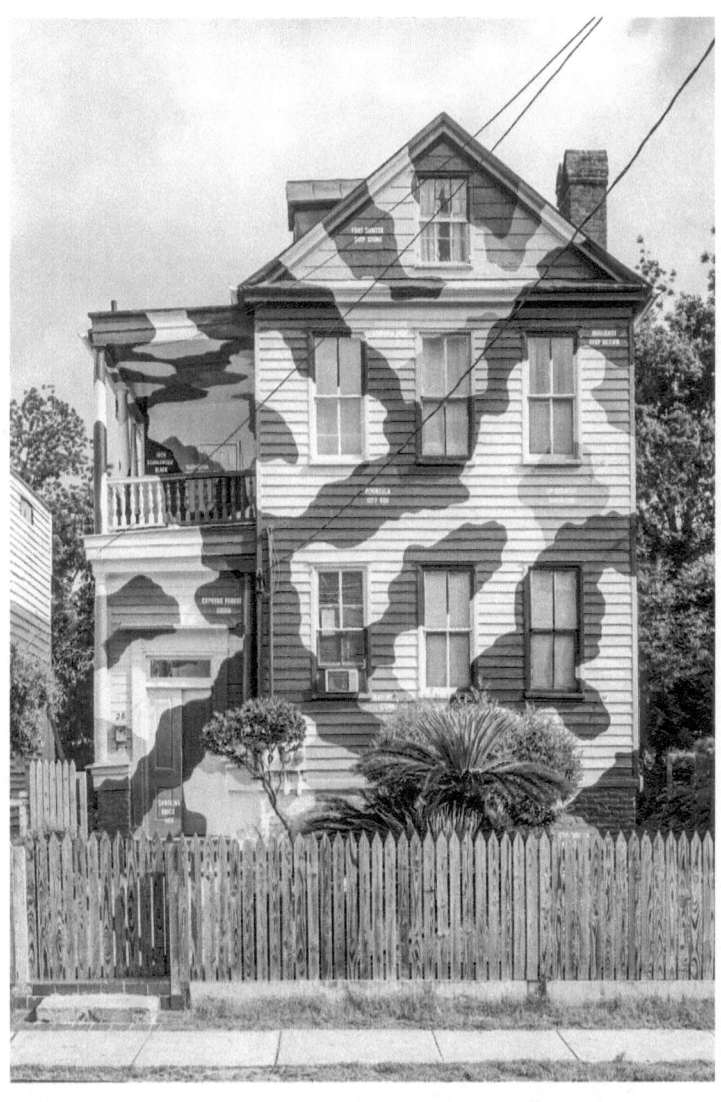

Kate Ericson and Mel Ziegler. *Camouflaged History*, 1991. *Places with a Past*, Charleston, South Carolina. Photo: John McWilliams, courtesy Spoleto Festival USA, Charleston, South Carolina.

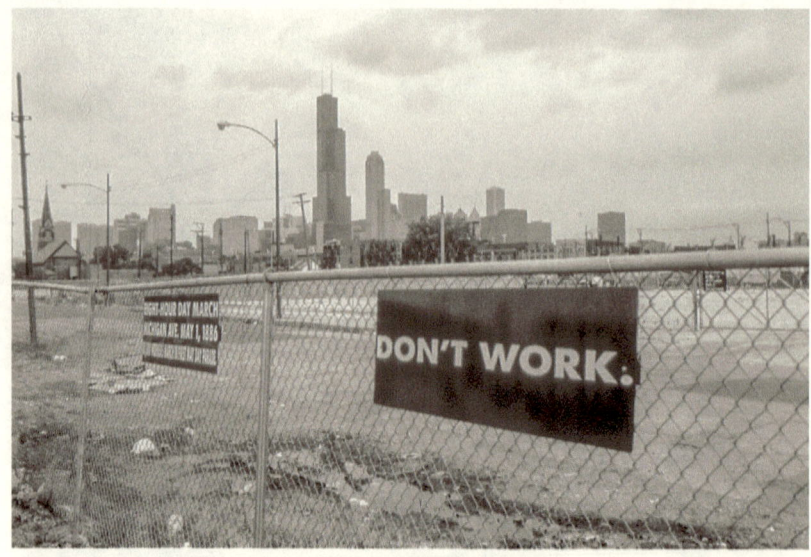

Daniel J. Martinez. *100 Victories/10,000 Tears*, 1993 (detail). *Culture in Action*, Chicago. Photo: John McWilliams.

them created work inside the Castle to be completed through direct interaction with visitors (what is today called participation); the other half worked outside in neighborhoods, and then resited these collaborative projects inside the Castle, seeking to communicate them meaningfully to spectators beyond the original local participants. Meanwhile, the city's social and cultural spheres, along with some from the arts field-at-large, convened around a program of dinners created with the Italian collective artway of thinking.

Curating those conversations led me to Dewey, but not until I had lived another multiyear project on the unlikely subject of contemporary art and Buddhism. That research initiative revolved around quarterly, three-day sessions at Green Gulch Zen Center, among fifty museum professionals brought together out of interest, not rank, and who sought to renew their commitment to opening up the experience of art to others.[7] Yet while Dewey's concept of art as experience lay behind the work of John Cage, Kaprow, and other contemporary artists being studied, we never got to him in our work that was, understandably, dominated by Asian sources.

Dewey remained unfinished business for me until this book project. My process has been decidedly curatorial. I began to study Dewey again for an exhibition around the rise of modernism in Chicago.[8] My focus was his shared mission with Jane Addams and his synchronicity of ideas with recent artist émigré László Moholy-Nagy. Next, as debates around social practice heated, artist and museum educator Pablo Helguera set out a challenge to tell Chicago's formative role in that story; so again another curatorial endeavor became a route to Dewey. He and Addams became the touchstones for the exhibition *A Proximity of Consciousness: Art and Social Action* and a series of books looking at Chicago's intermixing of art and activism since the 1880s.[9]

I must also share an early personal exposure to Dewey that prepared me to write this text. Growing up through public schools in New York, art was a regular, valued component. By adolescence, frequent trips to art museums turned into personal habit, reinforced by a faculty of high school art teachers. I must hasten to add that this was not some privileged situation; it was a regular working-to-middle-class school for that period: Deweyan. This early experience grounded me not just with knowledge but values that connected art to my every day and to my concept of public life. Without Dewey, I would not have found my way to art and the social opportunities it afforded, so different than those experienced by my parents and grandparents. Without Dewey, I would not have connected art to social justice, later finding curating as a way of life that would bring this into practice. Thus, as Dewey advocated, I write now from experience, because it is my lived experience that brings me to this task.

This book offers a thematic application of John Dewey's philosophy for contemporary artists, curators, and arts educators. Part 1 focuses on the internal development of the self; part 2 looks at external relationships in society. To Dewey, both paths are one as they take form within a conscious being. Chapter 1, "Making," explores why artists are intent on bringing forth works into the world. Dewey's understanding of this essential human impulse, through which civilizations have taken shape since the beginning of time, ignited his search for an American culture and its cultivation through the formation of the Works Progress Administration's Federal Art Project. Chapter 2, "Experiencing," places our experience of works of art within the larger framework of human interactions with the environment. In aesthetics, it is the experience that matters, so through Dewey's understanding we come to see that both the artist and viewer contribute to making art. Such aesthetic experiences enable us to make meaning and, thus, grow. Chapter 3, "Practice," looks at what it is to cultivate moments of growth and evolve one's work into a life practice. While this happens for artists, Dewey promotes the belief that we can all have a life practice, living our life as art.

Part 2 of this book examines the place of art in enabling us to act fully and justly in society. In chapter 4, "Democracy," individual expression comes up against collective concerns; we need to find balance to achieve the ideal of equality and be true to the common good. This is the art of democracy, a work-in-progress that demands our continual making. This, too, is the art of social practice: the practical experiments of artists who employ, as Dewey advocated, democratic means for democratic ends. In chapter 5, "Participation," we learn of Dewey's own lifetime of democratic actions, from his early activism in the Pullman Strike and his cocreation of some of the major social organizations of the twentieth century to his stewardship of Leon Trotsky's trial in Mexico City. This is paralleled by artists' organizational efforts toward productive change. As Dewey appreciated, forming such associations is not only a way of making social change but a way we understand what it is to be a public. Finally, the last chapter, "Communication," considers what it is for diverse peoples and interests to come together as a human community, through empathy and intellect. Art and aesthetic experiences foster greater consciousness of ourselves and others so as to enrich our sense of what it is to be alive and contribute to society.

In drawing upon Dewey's words throughout the book, I ask readers to bear in mind the philosopher's underlying belief in equality, in spite of the seemingly antiquated usage of the pronoun "he" and "man" to reference persons more broadly; he also uses "human organism" or "human being" and "race" to signify cultural or ethnic groups as well as the human species. I felt it was important to hear Dewey's voice and attune our listening to both his times and committed intent. Woven throughout this book are also the lived experiences and real insights of contemporary artists. They have come to my aid in articulating Deweyan ideas in contemporary art practice as they thoughtfully share their processes, demonstrating what it means to live one's art. By Dewey's definition, they fully participate, not just as cosmopolitan figures of the art world but also as persons in and of the world. I cannot thank them enough. They are voices worth hearing.

I would also like to acknowledge the steadfast efforts of my editor, Susan M. Bielstein, for suggesting the undertaking, being open to an old subject—John Dewey—then persevering with me to bring it to fruition. Jacquelynn Baas, Michael Brenson, and Mika Hannula were there from the beginning, offering encouragement in their belief that this was a worthwhile project. Ernesto Pujol was my artist-reader and, as a trusted friend, offered not only critical editorial comments but also his formidable writing acumen. I am also grateful to Susan Olin, whose copyediting improved this text immeasurably. Kate Zeller provided affirmations through our lived curatorial experiences together, and her insights along with those of Trevor Martin motivated the process. Finally, Elizabeth Smith and Claire Frost were superb researchers, and their enthusiasm in discovering Dewey gave me hope that this book might hold meaning for a new generation. Like Dewey, I will trust that the continuity of past, present, and future emerges in this book as we examine his critical legacy for democracy, so that contemporary readers find their place in this vital continuum.

PART ONE

The Artist's Process

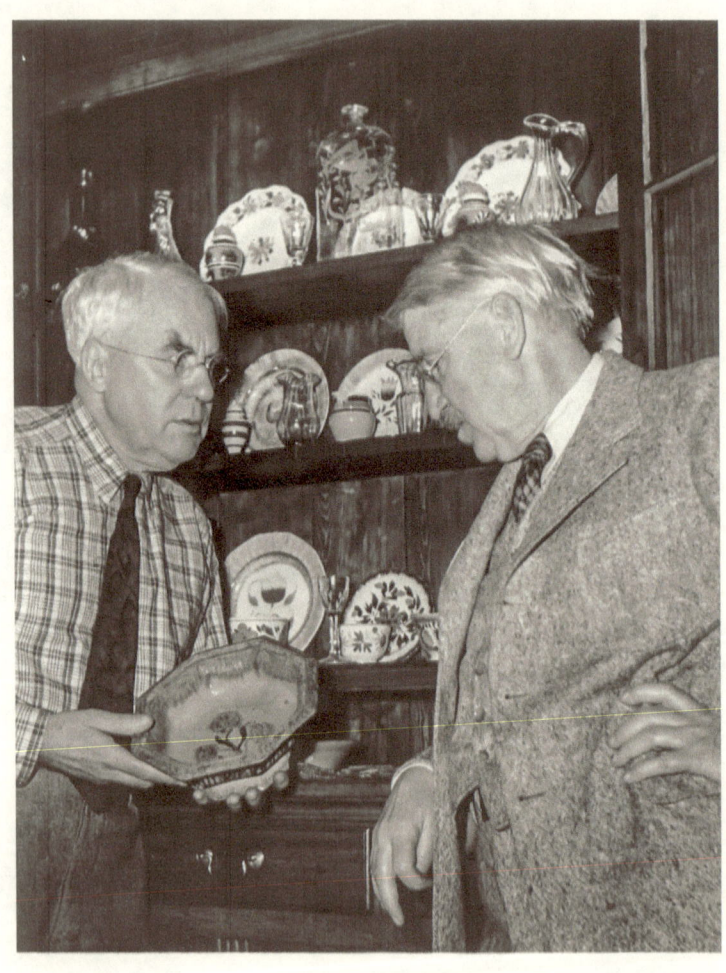

Philosophers John Dewey and Albert Barnes, n.d. Special Collections Research Center, Morris Library, Southern Illinois University, Carbondale.

1 Making

We are what we make. Dewey's revolution was to value the making. With that in mind, he attempted to construct a philosophy of life for a rapidly growing America in the throes of industrial and ideological change at the turn of the twentieth century. "I think the whole problem of understanding should be approached not from the point of view of the eyes, but from the point of view of the hands," he said.[1]

What is making? To Dewey, it was far more than bringing something into existence and giving it concrete form. We carry an interest through a process of inquiry. Care is invested, with the hope that something new can be achieved and the outcome will have been worth the effort. Making is vitalizing, Dewey observed, because it feels vitally important and can only be understood by carrying it out. The aliveness experienced by makers in the process derives from what they truly care about. Thus, the creative act is quite literally a life force.

Making is central to being an artist. During the process, the artist cares about bringing something to pass in an especially intense way, for a time, so focused that all else seems to fade from sight, so passionately possessed in the undertaking that the bounds of time and effort become irrelevant. During the making life feels uncharacteristically centered, and the calm that comes with clear intent sustains the uncertainty of creating something new. Projects (as many contemporary artists' work have come to be called) also carry this singular sense of searching that is renewed time and again with each new undertaking. And this happens, too, when collaborations are acts of comaking among dedicated and invested persons. Each party, as its knowledge is valued, sometimes for the first time, unlocks its own questions.

For a curator, the enterprise of exhibitions has a similar sensation: all-consuming, requiring gestation as well as concerted development, so that ideas can arise then be honed as one lives the project. So today curators care not only for the work entrusted to them but also for the shape of the show or project they make, expanding what is at the root of being a curator—*curare*—to care. This is a bond artists and curators share. It lives in their coevolution of ideas and shared, laser-sharp view into all the details of the enterprise that make each aspect urgently important at the moment of making.

Caring for Culture

Making is more than the province of the artist or craftsman or curator. Any work undertaken with care and attention by a committed, invested maker, can become art. "When we say that tennis-playing, singing, acting, and a multitude of other activities are arts, we engage in an elliptical way of saying that there is art in the conduct of these activities."[2] John Dewey even looked to his making as a philosopher: "Knowledge and propositions which are the products of thinking, are works of art, as much so as statuary and symphonies."[3] Art emerges as a quality of doing, and since it adheres to the manner of doing, art is adverbial in nature.

In 1934, Dewey wrote: "The intelligent mechanic[4] engaged in his job, interested in doing well and finding satisfaction in his handiwork, caring for his materials and tools with genuine affection, is artistically engaged. The difference between such a worker and the inept and careless bungler is as great in the shop as it is in the studio."[5] This creative potential inside everyone, not just those who identify as artists, was key to Dewey's philosophy of life and education decades before Joseph

Beuys pronounced "everyone is an artist." When, later still, Robert Pirsig thought back to the work of a couple of guys who messed up his bike's oil-delivery system in the 1974 classic *Zen and the Art of Motorcycle Maintenance*, he also uncannily built his case around the profession of mechanic: "they were uninvolved, had no identification with the job, were removed, and did not put care into what they did."[6] He further explained: a "person who sees Quality and feels it as he works is a person who cares. A person who cares about what he sees and does is a person who's bound to have some characteristics of Quality." And he cited, "The difference between a good mechanic and a bad one, like the difference between a good mathematician and a bad one, is precisely this ability to select the good facts from the bad ones on the basis of quality. He has to care!"[7] In the end, Pirsig determined the ill-suited mechanics were "spectators."[8]

As early as 1891, Dewey affirmed that each of us "is not born as a mere spectator of the world; [we are] born *into* it." We are each "an agent," he said, and if that is taken away, "nothing remains."[9] To be a maker is to be a participant. It is not just to take hand to material. Making is more than the physical labor. It is careful observation, precise thinking, "looking for the underlying form," Pirsig called it.[10] Martin Puryear is a sculptor who applies consummate craft as he arrives at a form; he is a maker who has broken barriers between art and craft, as well as what it is to be an African-American artist in the modern tradition. Yet when he publically spoke with Theaster Gates, he arrived at a perplexing point as he tried to understand the younger artist's expanded practice that spans from the studio to the boardroom to the street. Gates explained that the variety of things he creates is his work as an artist. This is not by fiat or conceptual ploy, but because of the care he puts into each aspect of his work. Seeing the threads that run through them and over time, he builds his life, with the parts reinforcing the whole. So working in multiple ways is about crafting the right project as he seeks to "resolve the right form for the right context." Then, no matter the shape the undertaking takes, "I get the same euphoric, artful feeling as being in the studio," he said.[11]

To Dewey, and later Pirsig, making goes to the core of our being: one must *be* a mechanic. To be a maker is to be fully engaged in what you are doing. Interests are at work, no matter how wide or idiosyncratically defined; they drive what you do, shape your intentions. While curiosity is an attribute, this word does not begin to capture the passion or urgency that comes from values that you hold dear at the very moment they are played out in the work and which cause what you do to be critically important to carry out and draw to conclusion. The maker, as a participant, values the doing as much or more than the thing done, and "does not shun moments of resistance and tension [but] rather cultivates them, not for their own sake but because of their potentialities, bringing to living consciousness an experience that is unified and total."[12]

Care, though this word speaks of skill and craft, of knowing how to do things well, is always about giving your full attention to the making. To Dewey, the maker undertakes an inquiry. It need not be revolutionary, a "first," but nonetheless it must be a discovery for you in the moment. No matter how many times you have been there, you do it anew. To do this, the maker has to be present in the moment, fully conscious. You live it. And this making is vital each and every time.

There is no doubt that Dewey's great respect for artists sprang from his sense that they assume this role out of necessity. To the philosopher, artists possess a keen ability to hear their inner voice and bring forth things into the world, while also continually challenging themselves to see in fresh ways, to locate resonant meanings, and to create change. To do so, artists occupy their own realm and control their means of production, even if they pay dearly for that freedom.

Dewey wanted this possibility for everyone. He thought if conditions were such that a worker could produce "articles of use that satisfy his urge for experience as he works," then psychological wisdom would tell us that that worker would beneficially gain in consciousness. In turn, such work would contribute to consumers' "heightened consciousness of sight and touch," offering small moments of aesthetic experience to us all.[13] But changing methods of mass production would require a "radical social alteration,"[14] because care was not an economic priority to those in power.

Embodied Making

For the maker, each work encompasses more than the thing itself. Working with wood to fashion furniture, maker-author Peter Korn writes: "The maker of craft (or any maker) is generally a lone individual asking, in part, how life may be lived with meaning and fulfillment. His work is a process of remapping social narratives central to human identity, so the things he makes speak to those issues."[15] Katie Paterson is working with a whole forest of trees in Oslo to make *Future Library*. It will be pulped in one hundred years from planting in order to print the manuscripts of authors commissioned once a year until then. Of making, she said:

> I treat my work like it was alive, a living being, sentient in some regard. Therefore, if alive, I must treat it with respect, care and compassion, for it to live and grow. This requires cultivation. I feel like I'm deceiving my work if it's made carelessly, overlooked, rushed. With *Future Library*, it more literally does live and grow; it needs to be tended with compassion over the years to come. I need to sustain strong willpower to see many of my works through. I must not only have belief but also compassion for the work: I must feel for it. I must always have a belief from the outset, that the work deserves to be brought into being—and I distinguish this belief from a value judgment on the work.[16]

As a work is brought into being, it becomes alive. And it lives in the maker. Pirsig, channeling Dewey, spoke of the integration:

> I've said you can actually see this fusion in skilled mechanics and machinists of a certain sort, and you can see it in the work they do. To say that they are not artists is to misunderstand the nature of art. They have patience, care and attentiveness to what they're doing, but more than this—there's a kind of inner peace of mind that isn't contrived but results from a kind of harmony with the work in which there's no leader and no follower. The material and the craftsman's

thoughts change together in a progression of smooth, even changes
until his mind is at rest at the exact instant the material is right.[17]

Making as a conscious act also develops the consciousness of the
maker. It is more than the workings of the brain or the muscle memory
of the hand. It is an embodied process of inquiry. Dewey believed that
the self can neither be separated into parts nor from its surroundings,
and with this he urged an understanding of the totality and continuity
of being. He called this concept mind-body. This feeling of unity within
and beyond the self contributes to artful making: "Any practical activity
will, provided that it is integrated and moves by its own urge to fulfillment, have esthetic quality."[18]

Creating art, or any invested making, draws upon the whole-and-
situated self, offering us an uncommon chance to feel a sense of wholeness within ourselves and connectedness to something beyond. We feel
a sense of completeness—not just of having completed a task. Korn
speaks from experience when he says: "Creative practice simply makes
our lives richer in meaning and fulfillment than they might otherwise be.
For some of us, creative practice may be among the few slender threads
that bind our lives together at all."[19] Furthermore, making as a manifestation of mind-body is a process by which we can further develop our
consciousness. What we make shapes the ethos of our life. Dewey surely
had Aristotle's *Ethics* in mind, seeking to bring into his own time the
ancient wisdom that to live well is to practice the values at the essence
of our being. Hence, having embodied these values, we act on them
through what we make.

If the workings of mind and body are unified, so too must be thinking and action, according to Dewey. But to suggest that all makers are
agents who think as well as act was problematic in his time. Class dis-
tinctions remained defined according to labor, with the intellectual elite
distinguished from the less-esteemed handworker, and the artist am-
biguously positioned between the two. Even today, art schools endeavor
to demonstrate that artists are researchers; this is consummated in artists' practice-based PhDs. But Dewey demanded no division between

theory and practice.[20] To him, the future depended on their union. So he wrote:

> The question of the integration of mind-body in action is the most practical of all questions we can ask of our civilization. It is not just a speculative question, it is a demand; a demand that the labor of multitudes now too predominantly physical in character be inspirited by purpose and emotion and informed by knowledge and understanding. It is a demand that what now pass for highly intellectual and spiritual functions shall be integrated with the ultimate conditions and means of all achievement, namely the physical, and thereby accomplish something beyond themselves. Until this integration is effected in the only place where it can be carried out, in action itself, we shall continue to live in a society in which a soulless and heartless materialism is compensated for by soulful but futile and unnatural idealism and spiritualism. For materialism is not a theory, but a condition of action; that in which material and mechanical means are severed from the consequences which give them meaning and value. And spiritualistic idealism is not a theory but a state of action; that in which ends are privately enjoyed in isolation from means of execution and consequent public betterment.[21]

Making as an embodied practice fulfills something basic to being human. As an evolutionary-minded philosopher, informed by the rising field of anthropology, Dewey was led to conclude that humans make things purposefully, in spite of variations across cultures. Thus, putting care into what we make, Dewey reasoned, must serve a purpose in living life. The answer he found lay in the satisfyingly invigorating moments in which meanings are made and which, in reaffirming our very aliveness, give us insight into how to operate in the world. Something else happens, too. We grow—and growth signals a healthy organism: we are not just alive but well.

We grow through learning, and making feeds the learning process. J. Morgan Puett is an artist who lives and learns through her art. When

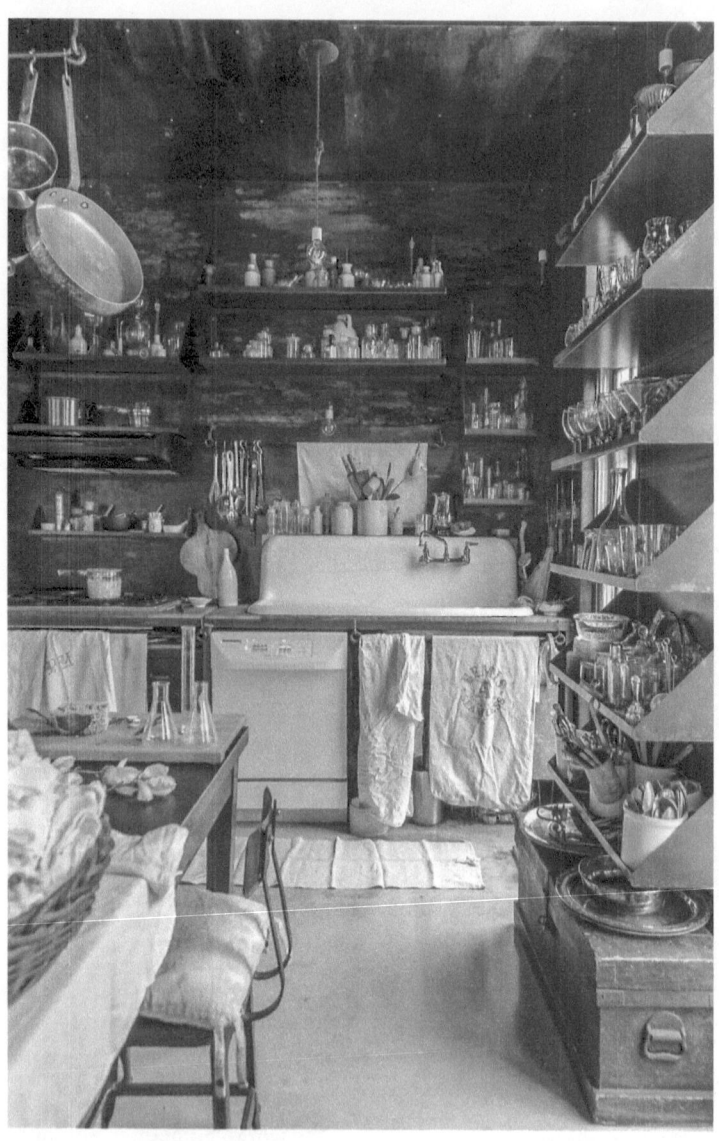

J. Morgan Puett. *Kitchen Laboratory*, 2007. Mildred's Lane, Beach Lake, Pennsylvania. Photo: Phil Mansfield.

artists like her say they are living their work, it is not merely an expression of working overtime; it is keeping the making present in all we do, even the ostensibly mundane. Then, we feel ourselves living life, growing and changing. "All art is autobiographical," says Puett, a Georgia native whose father practiced the art of breeding queen bees. "It's all about your experience and then trying to figure out what happened, not just being in touch with your feelings and gathering more experiences, but being driven by and producing from them." She continues:

> My father said, "As long as you're green, you grow; but when you think you're ripe, you begin to rot." I will always have that curiosity. I feel so incomplete, but that's also something I love about us as beings: that incompleteness. It's infinite. It involves all those questions about relations, the environment, living, and working. I want to learn more and a better way to do it all. I believe in generosity, sharing ideas. If we can't share ideas, we're doomed. I don't buy into capitalism and things like intellectual property—ideas you own and should not share— and that you can't work with your family and friends. I don't believe we're not supposed to do that. It's so important. As artists, work is our life; we have to weave our lifestyle through it. It is social and political engagement that embodies systems of labor: how we are, how we work together, our behaviors. Most importantly, it involves our relationship to the environment . . . how we behave on this planet. Being is the practice, and that is social and political.[22]

Dewey advocated just that. We may not be fortunate to have this on the job, but Dewey was clear: only through making our life is meaning made. He struggled with how to name this. He tried "occupation" but the connotation of employment was too restrictive. "Vocation" in his time was identified with manual training schools, yet he finally landed on this term. Derived from *vocare*, to call, *vocation* best conveyed the drive to do, as if told by a voice inside, and it came closest to his idea of a life's work.

Making that matters cannot be coerced. It only comes through volition, motivated by the values at stake for the maker. Dewey again used the example of the artisan whose education is more the acquisition of skills, but demands "observation, imagination, judgment, and even his emotions," writing:

> We should also have to say that the urge or need of an individual to join in an undertaking is a necessary prerequisite of the tradition's being a factor in his personal growth in power and freedom; and also that he has to see on his own behalf and in his own way the relations between means and methods employed and results achieved. Nobody else can see for him, and he can't see just by being "told," though the right kind of telling may guide his seeing and thus help him see what he needs to see. And if he has no impelling desire of his own to become a carpenter, if his interest in being one is perfunctory, if it is not an interest in being a carpenter at all, but only in getting a pecu-niary reward by doing jobs, the tradition will never of course really enter into and integrate with his own powers. It will remain, then, a mere set of mechanical and more or less meaningless rules that he is obliged to follow if he is to hold his job and draw his pay.[23]

What proved to be the essential idea and perhaps the greatest les-son of Pirsig's book, as foretold in its subtitle, *An Inquiry into Values*, is that you care about what has value to you; and to care about what you do, is to enact your values in what you make. Others often don't see why you make such an effort, so belief in the process requires con-viction, as Paterson tells. Along the way, artists invest all manner of re-sources—time, materials, ideas, emotions—without ever being assured of the rewards. Rather driven by whatever is their artistic inquiry at a given time, artists place great value on the search and are compelled to press forward, to get to a new place that will also open up more paths in the future and over a lifetime. The artist may be seen as an exception in this regard, someone whose output is unique in terms of the care that goes into the making. But to Dewey, this distinction only serves to sepa-rate the artist from other invested makers and, moreover, to separate art from the mainstream of life—setting it apart as exclusive and precious, a thing to be valued as an end in itself.

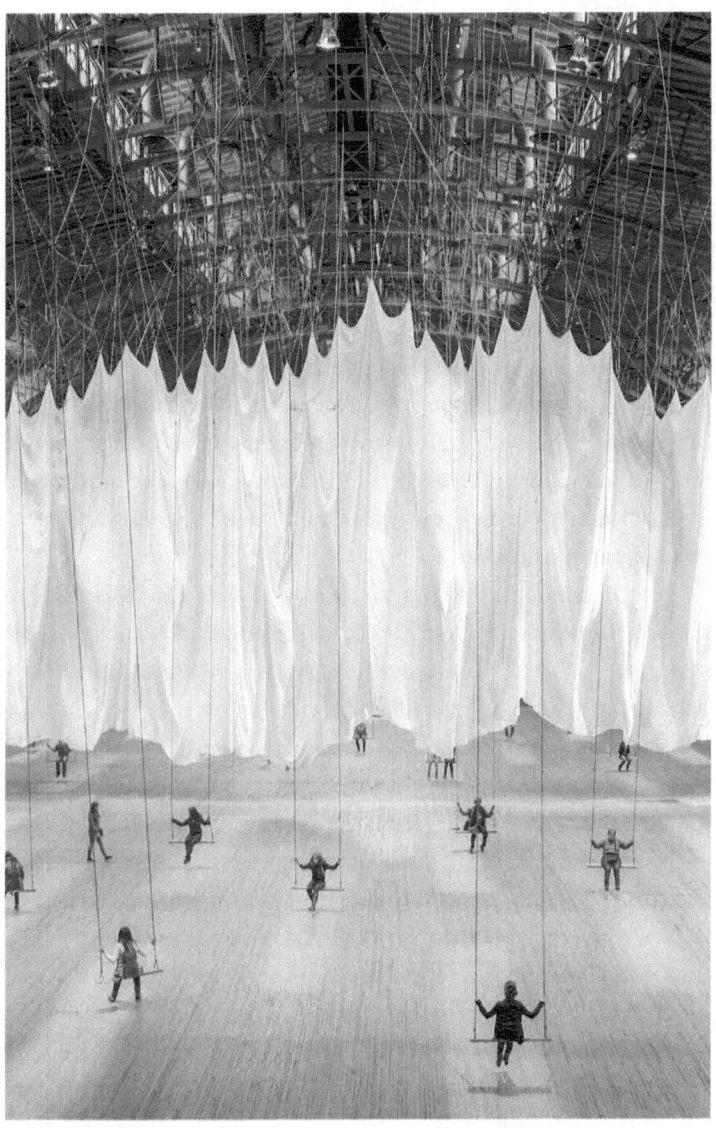

Ann Hamilton. *the event of a thread*, 2013. Park Avenue Armory, New York.
Photo: James Ewing/OTTO.

Time is not money. Dewey knew that art, that is, *all* making invested with care, suffers when put into a capitalist equation, so he emphasized that making must have value for the maker. He subscribed to a different equation: in expending energy, you gain energy. His model, moreover, was a perpetual cycle of inexhaustible energy by which makers generate energy for themselves — personal life energy — in the process of making. All the more amazing is that Dewey saw that, when works are made in this way, they generate energy for others. We feel this when in the presence of an object that has the quality of art (be it a work of fine art or not); we feel its presence, sensing the life investment of a maker who cared and was consciously present in the making. We share in the vitality of the work. While the values at stake for the maker may remain a mystery, we find value for ourselves. In this there is a sense of satisfaction, an affirmation of our own being, a realization of what we care about and value. We are participants.

Ann Hamilton is an artist who knows and feels this. In each of her projects, the body — hers, ours, or that of performers — is always present as the work is lived. Take *the event of a thread*, a title she adopted from Bauhaus artist-weaver Anni Albers.[24] It was an operatic work in scale and structure, whose sequential and simultaneous acts placed visitors at once in the role of participants and spectators. Its central element, a white satin curtain suspended at the height and stretching the width of the Park Avenue Armory, was human-powered by a series of swings and strings. Visitors' energy caused the constantly changing, fluid cloth to flow with the hypnotizing rhythm of slow-moving waves and (in a way unanticipated by the artist) causing many to lie down under it as if on the beach at the water's edge. It operated like a bellows, making air, giving oxygen, vitalizing everyone and everything around it. The work was alive, and it made those who were present feel alive as they both observed and continually made the work throughout the day until closing, only to be made again the next day by more visitors. Yet for this to occur, to make a space in which everyone can be a maker, Hamilton needed to ask herself, as she does each time she makes a new work — "What are the experiences that allow us to fall open to something, to pay attention?" — because she knows that with attention, consciousness expands.

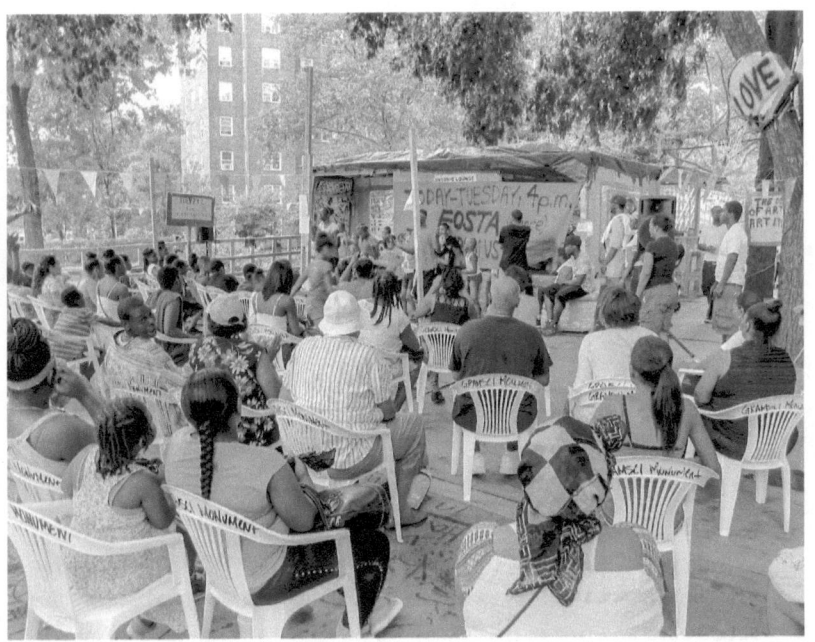

Thomas Hirschhorn. *Gramsci Monument, Running Event: "Fosta, From Us to All,"*
2013. Forest Houses, Bronx, New York. Photo: Romain Lopez, courtesy
Dia Art Foundation, Beacon, New York.

Working with others in a socially interventionist manner, Thomas
Hirschhorn has sited a series of vast projects in poor, working-class, or
migrant communities aimed to fuse political theory with everyday realities, creating works based on Baruch Spinoza in Amsterdam in 1999, on
Gilles Deleuze in Avignon in 2000, on Georges Bataille in Kassel's Turk-
ish guest-worker community in 2002, and lastly on Antonio Gramsci
in a primarily African-American housing project in the Bronx in 2013.
Like the previous editions, the New York work consisted of a series of
functional, living elements built by the residents according to the artist's
drawings, providing the community with a temporary archive, Internet
corner, library and exhibition space, lounge, radio station, workshop and
performance areas, and the Gramsci Bar.

Social practice artists are often confronted about the ethics of working in social contexts with people less advantaged than themselves; they

are challenged time and again with the question of who is the author. But Hirschhorn feels that the model of shared authorship is wrongheaded because it implies there is only 100 percent to be divided up and shared. So he invented the term "unshared authorship" to describe what he sees as a dynamic model with a multiplier effect, in which the potential to be a participant is unrestricted, and the project's quotient expands with each person who takes responsibility, so that there can be 1000% or more.[25] This is the generative notion of Dewey: to use energy to make more energy — and art is the ideal means.

Institutionalizing Making

When I walked away from spectator art toward a participatory public art practice in 1990, I was on a mission to break the institutional stranglehold on defining art and the art experience that I had experienced in my museum career. With the genre of institutional critique in vogue, this action became a part of that discourse. But at the same time I was seeking to expand the critical discourse around public art, still dominated by large-scale, outdoor sculptures. That was something I cared about, deeply. As I wrote of the process of curating *Culture in Action* in the early nineties: "Thus, from the start, issues that were meaningful to a specified population were the focus of the project. These audience-participants and the artists shared responsibility for the statements made. And the most in-depth and privileged experience of the art was not reserved for individuals privileged by wealth, reputation, or art knowledge, but was available to any who cared about the issues and wished to become involved."[26]

Framing art in museums through art history implied a feedback loop of producing more works and bigger art institutions, with no impact in other realms of life. Dewey knew that was wrong, and he knew it from experience. He served as inspiration for progressive institutions foregrounding the relevance of art to people in all walks of life. Most notable was the Newark Museum where, beginning in 1909, Director John Cotton Dana incorporated the commonplace into the collection. The Newark Museum developed a social mission to serve the community, reaching out to immigrant populations and becoming an educational resource. Nine years earlier, Dewey himself had experimented with this idea, collaborating with his close friend, settlement house founder Jane Addams. They instituted the Labor Museum in Chicago, which focused on forging links between Old World textile traditions and the city's modern industry to help bridge generational gaps in local immigrant families.

While American museums already by the end of the nineteenth century had welcomed in the masses, this gesture was at once generous and patriarchal, serving in part to flatter their benefactors, largely the newly moneyed striving for positions of cultural power (many of whom were the very factory owners Dewey witnessed eroding the human dignity of those they employed). So by the early 1930s the philosopher chided museums for proclaiming themselves to be the "proper home for works of art" and for isolating art by promoting "the idea that they are apart from the common life."[27] He blamed the overreach of capitalism for the establishment of museums in America and for the perception of art as "largely a form of commercialized industry in production of a class of commodities that find their sale among well-to-do persons desirous of maintaining a conventionally approved status."[28]

To Dewey, museums were quite literally evaporating the life out of art by showing art in a rarified context according to a contrived hierarchy of civilizations, with a lineage of makers and styles and litany of objects to be revered. He wrote, "the very perfection of some of the products, the prestige they possess because of a long history of unquestioned admiration, creates conventions that get in the way of fresh insight. When an art product once attains classic status, it somehow becomes isolated from the human conditions under which it was brought into being and from the human consequences it engenders in actual life-experience."[29] This, he believed, thwarted the real experience of art that transpires in the communion of viewer and object with the potential for transformative growth.

Defining culture on its terms, the museum canon denied multiple histories, as Dewey saw it, denigrating some works to privilege others, placing authored works above those by makers unknown, and separat-

ing fine art, craft, and the popular arts. So he took a political stance, concluding quite simply, "all ranking of higher and lower are, ultimately,
out of place and stupid. Each medium has its own efficacy and value."
In order to envision the art of the everyday, he promoted an open egali-
tarianism: "Whenever any material finds a medium that expresses its
value in experience — that is, its imaginative and emotional value — it
becomes the substance of a work of art."[30]

Dewey's urging of a reconsideration of the artfulness of useful things
and the usefulness of the so-called fine arts was grounded in his belief
that when art is closely connected with "the products of usual voca-
tions," then appreciation of works of art is "most keen."[31] Given a chance
to show what he meant, his top pick in the jury for the Museum of Modern Art's 1934 *Machine Art* show was an aluminum outboard propeller.[32]
But Dewey found his greatest ally in the cantankerous Alfred Barnes
who envisioned the museum as a place where the arts intermixed, realizing this in his display of hand tools and hardware, meticulously and
artfully placed between modern European and American paintings, and,
through his passion as an early collector of African art, widening the
geographic frame. There, at the Barnes Foundation, his factory workers
could come for instruction in art appreciation on paid time. Its gardens
offered visitors the chance to reflect on the relationship of art and nature. Barnes shared and debated his ideas on art with Dewey, and they
inspired each other in a shared mission of recasting cultural production
and its value for everyone irrespective of social standing.

When an art critic admonished me in 1992 during the process
of curating *Culture in Action* that the twelve Chicago Nestlé factory
workers participating in Simon Grennan and Christopher Sperandio's
candy bar project, *We Got It!*, would not become museumgoers, she only
had one kind of making in mind. But citing this same project, Arthur C.
Danto looked to it for what it revealed about the ontological meaning of community-based art projects, and in its constituency-specific
form found what he termed "*an art of their own.*" For Danto this raised
issues museums needed to contend with in contemporary, multicultural
America, fifty years after Dewey spoke out.[33] It was still important to
reaffirm the belief, as Dewey held, that art — in its making and in ex-

periencing it — does not exist in a closed, self-perpetuating system, relevant only to what Danto himself consecrated as the "art world." This was Dewey's gripe with museums, but if we become more aware of where artworks come from and what they can do, "we do not think of them as experiences we have to have by going to certain places, but that we may have at any time of day in connection with . . . objects, scenes, persons that are not in any way labeled to be works of fine art." [34]

Making Culture

Dewey envisioned his task as changing the field of aesthetics to "restore continuity between the refined and intensified forms of experience that are works of art and the everyday events, doings, and sufferings that are universally recognized to constitute experience . . . recovering the continuity of esthetic experience with normal processes of living." [35] His treatise *Art as Experience* came at a time ripe for change in the United States: the Great Depression. In 1935, just one year after the book was published, Dewey's long-held ideas about art and society proved fundamental to the launching of the Federal Art Project (FAP), a division of the Works Progress Administration (WPA). The approach of its director Holger Cahill depended on Dewey, whose ideas, he said, "probably more than those of any other philosopher of our time, have been taken as plans of action in the field of everyday activity." [36]

With the FAP Cahill sought to rectify the problem as Dewey saw it, that in "our modern industrial civilization, with its lack of unity, its tendency to divide various activities of life into separate grooves, the arts have been more isolated than ever before." Driven by the Dewey-inspired dream that in the US, free of an inherited aristocracy, art is no longer the domain of an elite class, Cahill wanted his efforts to result not only in "a better environment for the American artist," but also to "provide wider opportunities for the American people to participate in the experience of art." [37] Thus, the FAP could engender a more vital American culture.

Dewey believed that culture is "the ultimate judgment upon the quality of a civilization," [38] and he saw America lacking on this score.

If art can be a generator, in creating energy for the maker and giving energy to the viewer, then it can fuel society. At the inauguration of the FAP, Cahill spoke passionately of putting Dewey's ideas to work and making art part of the national agenda. "The emphasis on masterpieces is primarily a collectors' idea and is related to a whole series of commercial magnifications which have very little to do with the needs of society as creator or as participant in the experience of art." Now, thanks to Dewey, there were "greater resources of popular interest in the visual arts than at any other time in our history."[39] While some envisioned a new, wider presence for art, the establishment was not ready, as Dewey remarked:

> Even today many persons in the art field in Europe and America cannot go the whole democratic way in the arts. They cannot bring themselves to admit, somehow, that art, the highest level of creative experience, should belong to everybody. Many American artists, many American museum directors and teachers of art, people who would lay down their lives for political democracy, would scarcely raise a finger for democracy in the arts. They say that art, after all, is an aristocratic thing, that you cannot get away from aristocracy in matters of aesthetic selection. They have a feeling that art is a little too good, a little too rare and fine, to be shared with the masses.[40]

Instead the FAP considered the public a "participant in the experience of art,"[41] operating "on the principle that it is not the solitary genius but a sound general movement which maintains art as a vital, functioning part of any cultural scheme."[42] The FAP would encourage "the closest possible collaboration between the artist and the public for which he works," while retaining "the greatest degree of freedom for the artist."[43] And Dewey, too, for all his railing against art-for-art's sake, never sought to compromise artistic freedom or autonomy. In fact, he prized the artist's agency as a model for living. But by dissolving the distance between fine artists and other makers, Dewey sought to rehabilitate the existing image of the artist either as the lone visionary and exalted genius rising above the mundane, or as a solitary outcast. Both positions removed artists from life as it is lived, rendering them irrelevant to everyday concerns.[44] So, when American artists needed support during the Depression, it was because they, like those in so many other walks of life, made a contribution to the society in which we all live.

Putting 5,300 fine artists, craftsmen, commercial and applied artists to work, Cahill proudly declared the United States Government as "the greatest art patron"[45] — a claim unfathomable today. Seizing on Dewey's notion of material culture as evidence of the worth of a society, and believing that the US was no exception, he launched a campaign to show the value of America's cultural heritage at a time when European ideals still held sway among those of cultivated tastes and still dictated artists' educational paths. Sending hundreds of artists out into city and country between 1935 and 1942 to record the history of making, they created 18,000 watercolors of heretofore unrecognized works of furniture, woodcarving, baskets, coverlets, quilts, and much more. It was an "honest search for an art that mirrors the everyday experience, the sense and the sentiment of the American people."[46] The resulting Index of American Design became an unparalleled document of American culture.[47]

As an antidote to art elitism, the FAP valued making throughout the US. Cahill established "experimental galleries"[48] in parts of the country which had never had spaces to show art, places which were beginning to assemble their own narratives through local artifacts, an impulse carried on in the creation of museums of Americana east and west. And Dewey was there.[49] This wide geographic reach also meant trained artists did not need to uproot to a handful of metropolitan centers or flee to Europe, but were encouraged to find ways to contribute to the environment that had nurtured and inspired them. For others, Cahill's Community Art Center program spawned scores of opportunities for anyone interested to engage, giving the public direct access to making and seeing art irrespective of their social standing or level of skill. Founded with the aim of building a broad public for art, these centers reached deep into communities.[50]

With an art for and by the people, *an art of their own*, Cahill challenged the notion of who can be an artist and demonstrated that when making happens more broadly and culture is not reserved for the few, or

seen in only selective places, or accessed only on special occasions, we all
benefit. Herein the FAP communicated democratic values. To Dewey,
this became all the more urgent as social freedoms in European countries, long upheld as models of culture, began to wither under totalitarian regimes. Writing of this in his 1939 volume *Freedom and Culture*,[51] he
took this theme further the following year in his advocacy of the FAP,
saying:

> As a symbol, the work carried on by the Section of Fine Arts is a ser-
> vice to democracy, so important, even in its present comparatively
> limited scale, that to starve it or allow it to lapse would be a defeat for
> democracy as genuine as one taking place on a physical battlefield.
> For the same reason, this governmental activity is more than a symbol.
> Hundreds of thousands of persons all over this broad land now have
> opportunities to see and enjoy works of art which they had not before.
> They are developing, within themselves, germs that were part of their
> being but which never had a chance, because of lack of nourishment,
> to grow.
>
> If the arts come forth from museums to which they have retired,
> if they become a living part of the walk and conversation of the aver-
> age man, and thereby parts of the legitimate heritage of a democratic
> people, a great debt will be owed to the stimulus provided by this
> governmental section in the buildings which belong to the common
> people and where they daily assemble.
>
> Old World countries have been able to develop the fine arts by
> means of the patronage of the nobility and the wealthy. Their healthy
> development in our country will depend upon the active response of
> the civic consciousness of the common people.[52]

Though he strongly endorsed the work of the FAP, Dewey felt the
WPA's social programs did not go far enough, and he did not mind telling Franklin Delano Roosevelt. Yet in the end the WPA lasted only eight
years. By 1943, it was over and with it the FAP. We did not see this potential reawakened again until 1965, with the formation of the National Endowment for the Arts (NEA), one of a series of social reforms that led

off with the Civil Rights Act the prior year. President Lyndon B. John-
son, in his inaugural statement, spoke in Deweyan fashion: "In the long
history of man, countless empires and nations have come and gone.
Those which created no lasting works of art are reduced today to short
footnotes in history's catalogue."[53] But the NEA's support of individual
artists, a boon in the form of direct grants, smacked of artists on the dole.

Finally it was charges of immorality that brought NEA funding to a
screeching halt in 1995. The diversification of cultural representation, so
richly explored during the multicultural eighties and early nineties, had
so enlarged the view of who is an American and what is American culture that the Conservative Right closed in. Arts writer Michael Brenson
saw an attempt to regain ground wrongheadedly further institutionalize
the art world, "separating the social value of art from the courage and
personalities of the artists who make it."[54] And further echoing Dewey
of long ago, he also blamed museums for seizing the moment for their
own ends:

> They want to be able to use art as their boards of trustees, economic
> advisors, and curators direct them to ... to use art to advance their
> social status, economic aura, global ambition, and brand name with-
> out any obligation to consider the realities of its makers or the condi-
> tion of the artist in America. By separating art from the artist's body,
> Congress and the NEA made it easy for art to be institutionally per-
> ceived as weightless and portable property, like a stock, or a bond, or
> an image that could be instantaneously called by and manipulated or
> marketed on the Web.[55]

The agency has always had to tread a fine line in a country where art
seems indulgent, elitist, without use. Personal expressions, so the reasoning goes, ought to live and die like any other product in the market-
place.[56] But for Dewey, when we make art, when we truly care for what
we do, there is a dual effect: we participate in further realizing who we are
as individuals, and, communicating through our work to others, we gain
the potential to further realize ourselves as we make meaning. When we
look to the 1930s, to artists employed by the FAP as a union of cultural

workers creating a civic patrimony, to this nation's history of creative production as catalogued for the first time in the Index of American Design, and to the thousands of youth and adult learner-makers who populated community art centers across the country and across class, we see the value of making in action. Yet defending the value of art in ordinary life remains an American challenge.

Brenson concludes his 2001 missive on the artist with questions that are as true now as when he asked them, and as when Dewey and Cahill before him took up their inquiry:

> How can the aesthetic experience be known sufficiently to allow the intensity of perception and emotional courage that often accompany it at its most profound to clarify and deepen our relationship with one another? How can that quality of awareness and mind that can be developed through the making and experiencing of art inform everyday life? How can the astounding and dynamic interconnectedness of the creative process give artists and their audiences a surer sense of place, both within themselves and in their multiple worlds? These are aesthetic questions, political questions, ecological questions, questions which artists and the people who believe in them need to feel at home.[57]

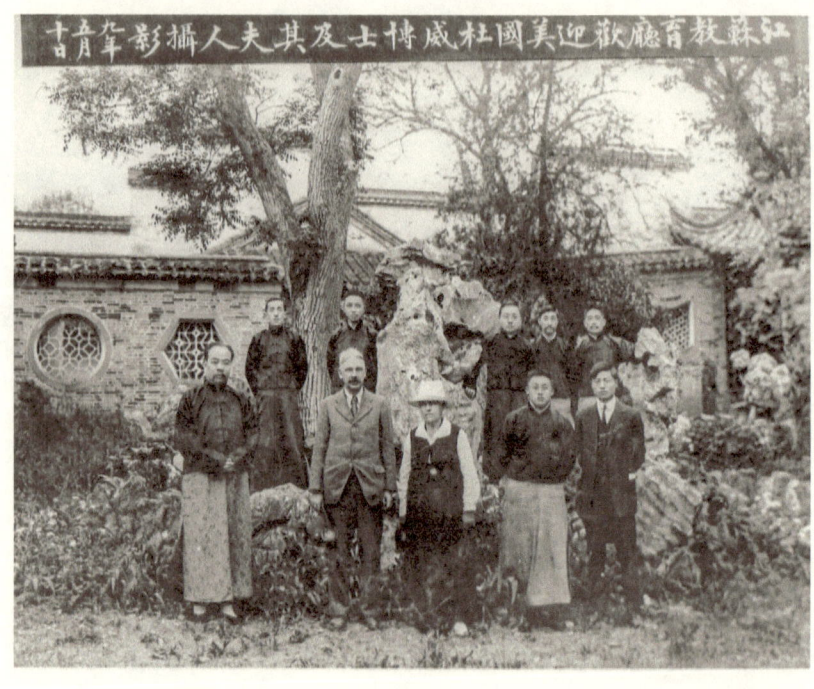

Alice and John Dewey with Jiangsu educators, Jiangsu Province Department of Education, May 10, 1920. Nanjing, Jiangsu Province, China. Special Collections Research Center, Morris Library, Southern Illinois University, Carbondale.

2   Experiencing

Talking with Rirkrit Tiravanija, he shared, "for me, art is more about the energy that one is able to make other people feel. I think when I speak of energy or the idea of self-sufficiency, which is self-motivated, it's almost like where you can see the art happening." We were listening to Rick Lowe, whose Project Row Houses had transformed the Third Ward in Houston by renovating a group of working-class shotgun houses into artist-residency sites, temporary homes for single mothers, and community spaces, creating a model for social sustainability through art. Afterward Rirkrit said:

> Rick talked about watching a man who comes to mow the grass around Project Row Houses. This man comes with his mower and spends his time taking care of the lawn without being asked or paid. From what he was saying, Rick looks at this in a certain way; he feels the energy of that man. It's an energy that you get that's very generous, and it's generous because it is immersive. It is something this person is doing with a kind of spirit and energy that is very real. It isn't something done in passing. It's something that he will always do and be. I think in a way I have always wanted to just trim the lawn, but with the kind of spirit and energy that makes people see bigger things than that, you know?[1]

I had heard Rick talk about other individuals in his neighborhood who had caught his attention. He had spoken of their dignity and worth in the community and his desire to honor them, working with them to bring forward their own potential in crafting their path in life. This mutual way of experiencing is the way Rick described people's reactions to Project Row Houses:

> Everybody is not going to experience it the same way — everybody doesn't experience a painting the same way or a sculpture the same way. And so we try to create an aesthetic vibe, an aesthetic experience, with people within the context of the neighborhood whether they're connected with any of the programs or not. They may not necessarily know the connectedness of things, but there's something they find that's valuable for them. And sometimes that value is reflected back to us in ways that heighten our awareness of things that we're doing that are working, or it heightens our awareness of where there are gaps and holes where we need to explore. So part of it is about having a sense of connectedness with people, but the other part is about generating an opportunity for people to have an experience that heightens their ability to be aware in the place that they are in so that they can contribute in their own ways.[2]

In the presence of the man with the mower, Rick and Rirkrit saw someone who lived his life as a participant, taking care and doing what he does as an art. And Rick's aesthetic experience of this act of mowing triggered an aesthetic experience in Rirkrit as Rick retold the story. It connected each of them to something deeper within themselves, and to something wider in the world.

Dewey's Aesthetic Experience

Dewey defined aesthetic experience simply as *an* experience. Slight as this may sound, he realized that experience cannot be fully expressed in words. Language has its limits.[3] Experience has to be experienced. Yet *an* experience is more than a passing moment or incident; it enters consciousness and carries with it the potential for meaning and growth in awareness. It has a depth of feeling, and Dewey valued feelings as holistic expressions of the mind-body. In *Art as Experience* he wrote:

> In such experiences, every successive part flows freely, without seam and without unfilled blanks, into what ensues. At the same time there is no sacrifice of the self-identity of the parts. . . .
>
> An experience has a unity that gives it its name, *that* meal, that storm, that rupture of friendship. The existence of this unity is constituted by a single quality that pervades the entire experience in spite of the variation of its constituent parts. This unity is neither emotional, practical, nor intellectual, for these terms name distinctions that reflection can make within it.[4]

For Dewey, only aesthetic experience has this quality of unity: it is definitional. He had taken up the subject of the unity of experience already in 1919, saying: "When experience is aligned with the life-process and sensations are seen to be points of readjustment, the alleged atomism of sensations totally disappears." But philosophers had constructed "elaborate Kantian and post-Kantian machinery" to understand experience, so Dewey took exception to his own field, as he often did, pointing to the agency we all have in regard to this subject: "Experience carries principles of connection and organization within itself. These principles are none the worse because they are vital and practical rather than epistemological. . . . This organization intrinsic to life renders unnecessary a super-natural and super-empirical synthesis. It affords the basis and material for a positive evolution of intelligence as an organizing factor within experience."[5]

A decade later, he drew upon science to help make his point on unity:

> . . . the conclusion of Einstein, in eliminating absolute space, time, and motion as physical existences, does away with doctrine that statements on space, time and motion as physical existence . . . [and] compels the substitution of the notion that they designate *relations*

of events. As such relations, they secure ... the possibility of linking
together objects viewed as events in a general system of linkage and
translation. They are the means of correlating observations made at
different times and places ... they do the business that all thinking
and objects of thought have to effect: they connect, through relevant operations, the discontinuities of individualized operations
and experiences into continuity with one another.[6]

When we have *an* experience, we sense a greater unity as we make meaning, making connections within and beyond ourselves. Aesthetic experience flows from life as we live it and, through us, into the lives of others.
This is the natural order of things.

Dewey offered two criteria by which we can gauge whether an experience is aesthetic or not. First, is it complete, what he called *consum-
matory*, and has it reached a conclusion? Second, is it integrated within
you—is it something you have taken into your life and made part of
who you are, and did it allow you to reconsider life more thoughtfully?
Dewey summed it up this way: "We have *an* experience when the material experienced runs its course to fulfillment. Then and only then is it
integrated within and demarcated in the general stream of experience
from other experiences."[7]

Dewey identified aesthetic experience in two forms: the primary,
as it is experienced in the course of daily life, and the rarefied, as it is
experienced in works of art. The wider, primary form happens in acts
of making, all kinds of making when undertaken with care. It also occurs in the course of our interactions with nature, people, ideas, all sorts
of things when "a body of matters and meanings, not in themselves esthetic, *become* esthetic." The second, rarefied form, occurs when we encounter works of art and, acting on us, we are in some way affected. Thus,
art is a form of experience because it "unites the very same relation of
doing and undergoing, outgoing and incoming energy, that makes an
experience be an experience."[8] And Dewey goes further to clarify this
relationship between the art experience and life experiences that can be
aesthetic. He writes: "The arts and their aesthetic experience are inten-
tionally cultivated developments of this primary aesthetic phase." Aes-

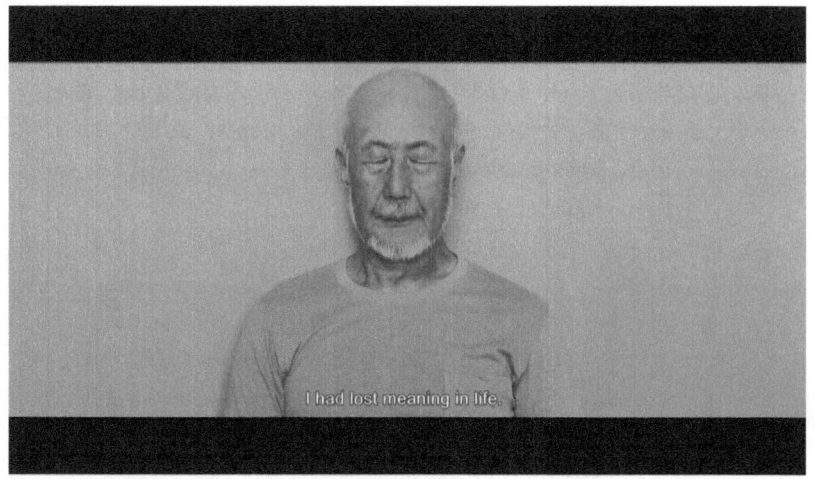

I had lost meaning in life.

Jeon Joonho. *About Beauty*, 2013. Single-channel video with sound, 4 min., 35 sec.
Photo: Courtesy of the artist.

thetic experience of this order arises "out of what is natural and spontaneous in primary experience," and therefore, "in all probability, [it] is the
simplest and most direct way in which to lay hold of what is fundamental
in all the forms of experience."[9]

Dewey proclaimed that art is "the most direct and complete manifestation there is of experience *as* experience."[10] And within this we find
his most radical assertion: art is not the thing but the experience; it "is
a strain in experience rather than an entity in itself." He endeavored to
explain: "In common conception, the work of art is often identified with
the building, book, painting, or statue in its existence apart from human
experience. Since the actual work of art is what the product does with
and in experience, the result is not favorable to understanding."[11]

Now this could well be seen as devaluing the art object, and many
an art career is built on the commerce of objects. So, one need look no
further to see that Dewey's perception of art posed a challenge both to
art history and criticism and to the art system, then and now. But Dewey
was committed to the appreciation of life experiences that give rise to
aesthetic experience because he knew—from experience—that it is
these moments that make life worth living. This is what Jeon Joonho

shows us in his short film called *About Beauty*. It was his attempt to explain aesthetic experiences for which he had no words. To do so, he asked his father to tell his life story. In less than five minutes, the older man, eyes closed as if in a dream state, seeks to arrive at the essence of his own passage from youth to retirement, from purposefulness to meaninglessness, then offers in reflection:

> When you grow old, you sleep less. . . . So if I woke up around dawn,
> I wandered around here and there climbing the hill at the back of my
> house and walking along the beach. Then one morning, I had climbed
> up Bongrae Mountain just back here and was resting on a rock. Ah!
> The sun was rising from the sea over there. It was truly a spectacular
> sight. It's still vivid in my mind. It was as if the whole sea was on fire.
> As I watched the blazing sun rise, I thought it was extremely beauti-
> ful. And it came to me at that moment. I am able to see this beautiful
> scene because I am alive. Why hadn't I appreciated this beauty until
> now? I was thankful that I was alive. I know that I don't have long to
> live. However, I'm not afraid of death. If I'm afraid of something, it
> is the fact, and I'm sad, that I don't have much time left to see these
> things.[12]

And with those words, the artist's father opened his eyes.

While this film conveys a life experience of Jeon's father that was an aesthetic experience of the first order, it offers us an aesthetic experience of the second, more rarified order through an artwork. It is "the outcome of a skilled and intelligent art of dealing with natural things for the sake of intensifying, purifying, prolonging and deepening the satisfactions which they spontaneously afford," as Dewey said of the nature of art itself. And in doing so, art generates energy that is one with the life force of all existence, for, as he also said: "That, in the process, new meanings develop, and that these afford uniquely new traits and modes of enjoyment is but what happens everywhere in emergent growths."[13]

Dewey took great exception to "*theories* which isolate art and its appreciation by placing them in a realm of their own, disconnected from other modes of experiencing," stating that "a philosophy of art is sterilized unless it makes us aware of the function of art in relation to other modes of experience."[14] Always seeking to bridge the two, he adds that these two kinds of aesthetic experience have been "traditionally (but fallaciously) regarded as so many different, separate, isolated, independent divisions of subject matter."[15] Not only are art and life related, but Dewey also believed that "in order to *understand* the esthetic in its ultimate and approved forms," by which he meant its form as works of art, "one must begin with it in the raw; in the events and scenes that hold the attentive eye and ear of man."[16]

Thus, the philosopher reasoned — and felt — that just as an experience of something in life (like seeing a sunrise) can be transformed into a work of art, our experience of works of art can become part of life as they become absorbed or reignited in us. He asserted, "a work of art no matter how old and classic is actually, not just potentially, a work of art only when it lives in some individualized experience." And because "experience is a matter of the interaction of the artistic product with the self," a given work of art "is recreated every time it is esthetically experienced"[17] by each individual. Moreover, over time, as we bring new experiences to the same work, our experience of it can change. This dynamic nature of art is so alive in us that we can even experience a work of art when no longer in its presence. Once an art experience is consummated by and integrated into us, it remains open to new experiences that can trigger and bring it back into consciousness.

Dewey prized art as the most energetic form of experience, attributing this to the conscious intent of the artist. When Katie Paterson employs a forest of spruce trees and library of books to make *Future Library*, it is not as an avant-garde gesture but as a reinvestment in the world around us through art. Her material elements gain in aesthetic presence for the very reason that we know them in so many other normative ways. As the meanings unfold, they tap into the extraordinary in the ordinary. The duration required to grow a forest suggests it is worth investing in the future, expressing the hope that humanity will survive another hundred years and more, while satisfying our longing to communicate beyond our allotted time. *Future Library* also reminds us (as Dewey would appreciate) that both forest and library are public as-

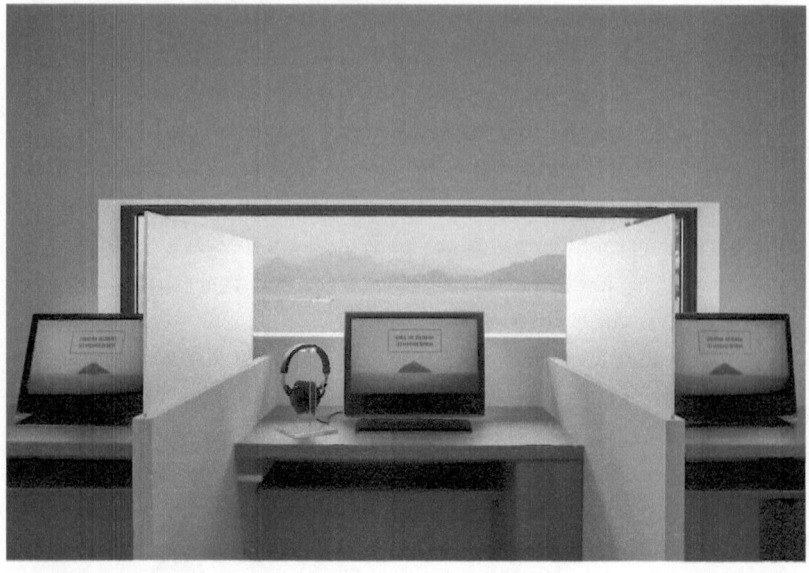

Christian Boltanski. *Les Archives du Coeur* (*The Heart Archive*), 2008–ongoing.
Installation at Teshima Island, Japan. Photo: Kuge Yasuhide. Courtesy of Fukutake
Foundation, Benesse Art Site Naoshima, Japan.

sets that we hold in common and for the common good. Locating such
meanings in this work, it creates in us the sense of unity which Dewey
believed characterized all true aesthetic experiences.

Paterson's work creates *an* experience for the very reason she used
common elements, then brings them to our attention, making us see
them anew. In this way *Future Library* becomes a compound aesthetic
experience: on the one hand, primary in the use of actual aspects of life,
and, on the other, refined as an intentional work by an artist. In the end
it is both experience as art *and* art as experience.

I had a chance to experience Christian Boltanski's *Heart Archive* on
Teshima Island. It is an ongoing project of heartbeats recorded around
the world during his exhibitions, then collected as an expanding, pulsat-
ing library on this remote island in Japan. And there I logged in and lis-
tened to my son's heartbeat, which he had contributed a few years prior
when the project took place in New York City. Why is such a simple
thing like a heartbeat so extraordinary? Is it that its existence is deeply

reassuring? Surely it was, in my experience, while looking over the bank of computers out the window and across the Inland Sea. That computer, so many names and heartbeats, and the water were specific yet completely familiar. Yet Boltanski's genius time and again is the ability to use the common and mundane to enable us to enact our humanity; that human energy attracts us, pulls us into the work, nourishes, and perplexes us. Ultimately, it fulfills a need to connect.

Then there is the case of the artfulness of socially engaged art practice. Artists' use of life processes as art processes has been much disputed or not seen as art at all. By contrast, I think Dewey would have given this development in contemporary art an über-aesthetic experience status. More than offering one of two ways of having aesthetic experience, that is, the primary form in life or the specialized way in art; and instead of creating a dual experience of art and life as does Paterson or Boltanski, social practice fuses the two into one inseparable union. There is a direct transmission of experience at an aesthetic level.[18]

I believe the resistance to recognizing how we *actually* experience social practice art stems from the art field's perpetual distancing of art from life, insisting on the same separation Dewey saw as misguided. But the philosopher reminds us that, in both the primary and in the art strain, "the material of esthetic experience in being human—human in connection with the nature of which it is a part—is social."[19] So more than other art genres in which we can draw upon our experience to make meaning, with social practice our past and present are marshaled to give rise to aesthetic experiences. And this is true even of a project we have not been a part of or seen on the ground: we can have *an* experience of it because of experiences we have lived. These may have been aesthetic experiences at the time we had them, or not, but in the encounter with a social art project our life experiences are called upon to arise aesthetically, perhaps for the first time, and that can be profound.

When we have *an* aesthetic experience, we experience the world in a revitalized way, Dewey tells us. Therefore, it should not be surprising that as socially engaged art goes directly to the source—to life itself—drawing out the aesthetic experiences that the everyday affords and bringing life for a time into the frame of art, we can have experiences that are meaningful and transformative. With openness, such aesthetic experiences lead to new understandings of ourselves, the world, and our place in it. But for this, consciousness is essential.

Experiencing Consciousness

Aesthetic experience helps us live life more consciously. It plies the cycle of experience as it moves through life, intensifying and thus making our experiences more satisfying, so we may live more fully. As Dewey saw it: "Experience, in the degree in which it *is* experience, is heightened vitality. Instead of signifying being shut up within one's own private feelings and sensations, it signifies active and alert commerce with the world; at its height, it signifies complete interpenetration of self and the world of objects and events." Contrary to what we might think at first mention, these "biological commonplaces" (as Dewey called them) through which a life responds to its environment and grows, are something more: "they reach to the roots of the aesthetic in experience."[20] Transformative aesthetic experience triggers growth.

In her performance at Fukushima, Eiko Otake sought to embody its nuclear tragedy. She told choreographer and dancer David Brick: "I don't believe in the grand gesture," slowly sweeping her arm over her head. "Suddenly and softly her arm stopped halfway," Brick records. Then Eiko added, "in every movement there must be hesitation." Brick calls this the "politics of hesitation," suggesting "a pause in time, consideration, self-questioning, opening wider to the moment."[21] As an embodied maker, too, he recognizes how awareness affects his perception of everything around him, offering this description of a Deweyan, primary, aesthetic experience of heightened consciousness:

> One day you wake up and everything is interesting. You walk to the subway, or you go to work, and everything you see delights you. You are curious and content about everything. The old man and middle-aged woman carefully cleaning the gutters in the subways; the way the light stripes the streets with the shadows of buildings. Your stomach growling, loud enough to make someone look up, makes you laugh.

But this day is an ordinary day, and nothing momentous has changed in your life. You didn't get a promotion or win an award. You haven't broken up with a lover or heard from an old friend. You haven't just had a daughter or had a big insight into your problems at work. Nothing special is happening but all around the world glows.[22]

Aesthetic experience happens when we are open and aware of our environment. But it is all a matter of perception. Dewey made a distinction between perception and recognition. With the latter "we fall back ... upon some previously formed scheme," so that then recognition enables us to go about our day. It is a mechanism that is often unconscious. But when "perception replaces bare recognition ... consciousness becomes fresh and alive"; it is "an act of the going-out of energy in order to receive, not a withholding of energy."[23]

As consciousness arises at the level of heightened awareness, it "takes up into itself meanings covering stretches of existence wrought into consistency." Yet this does not happen quickly, Dewey tells us. "It marks the conclusion of long continued endeavor; of patient and indefatigable search and test. The idea, in short, is art and a work of art. As a work of art, it directly liberates subsequent action and makes it more fruitful in the creation of more meanings and more perceptions."[24]

Perception was at the root of making for pioneer performance artist Allan Kaprow, a thoughtful reader of Dewey, who chose to use life actions to create his happenings, a participatory approach that liberated art from the gallery in order to be of and in the world. It was social, or as Dewey might have said, a "widely human" practice. Experience was his medium, as Jeff Kelley tells it: Kaprow "attend[ed] as an artist to the meanings of experience instead of the meanings of art (or 'art experience'). Because the meanings of life interest[ed] him more than the meanings of art, Kaprow positioned himself in the flux of what Dewey called 'the everyday events, doings, and sufferings that are universally recognized to constitute experience.'"[25] And Kelley notes that on page 11 of Kaprow's copy of *Art as Experience*, he underlined: "Even a crude experience, if authentically an experience, is more fit to give a clue to the intrinsic nature of esthetic experience than is an object already set apart from any other mode of experience."[26] So Kelley concludes that for Kaprow the aim was "consciousness in its fullest sense. This sense of fullness is probably what Dewey found esthetic about experience."[27]

Because aesthetic experience is consummated and integrated, it brings us to consciousness. But to achieve this, Dewey knew we need to attune our perception. Zen Buddhism opened up the way for Kaprow to perceive.[28] In Zen, the common everyday is the way. It is the "*immediate experience* of what, at the bottomless ground of Being, cannot be apprehended by intellectual means and cannot be conceived or interpreted even after the most unequivocal and incontestable experiences: one knows it by not knowing it," writes Eugen Herrigel in *Zen in the Art of Archery*, a conscious memoir.[29] Dewey himself, seeking to express the integral nature of experience, resorted to a koan-like explanation: "Mountain peaks do not float unsupported; they do not even just rest upon the earth. They *are* the earth in one of its manifest operations." Elsewhere he evoked what might be seen as the image of meditation as he explained the oneness of experience: "Experiencing like breathing is a rhythm of intakings and outgivings."[30]

Although Dewey knew about Buddhism and crossed paths in Chicago and Japan with the key proponent of Zen in the US, D. T. Suzuki, he was not a practitioner, as was Kaprow. Instead of meditation, Dewey used art, because for him art was an equally ideal way to cultivate consciousness. "The artist's experiments 'open new fields of experience and disclose new aspects and qualities in familiar scenes'" and, like all aesthetic experiences, they repay us by nurturing consciousness within us. Dewey wrote, "What is intimated to my mind, is, that in both production and enjoyed perception of works of art, knowledge is transformed; it becomes something more than knowledge because it is merged with non-intellectual elements to form an experience worthwhile as an experience."[31] All making offers a sense of unity for the maker and the viewer when undertaken as an art. Aesthetic experiences communicate that unity.

The Viewer's Experience

Each one of us embodies aesthetic experience. The experience of art rests with the one having it. Just what this means has been dissipated through adages such as "beauty is in the eye of the beholder" or "to each his own interpretation," overriding the authority of art professionals. But Dewey recognized the profundity of experience in both the making and viewing of art. On one side, the "artist embodies in himself the attitude of the perceiver while he works."[32] On the other, in order to have *an* aesthetic experience, we must take the work into our own being through a perceptual creative act akin to that of the artist:

> To perceive, a beholder must create his own experience. And his creation must include relations comparable to those which the original producer underwent. They are not the same in any literal sense. But with the perceiver, as with the artist, there must be an ordering of the elements of the whole that is in form, although not in details, the same as the process of organization the creator of the work consciously experienced. Without an act of recreation the object is not perceived as a work of art.[33]

Later, he added:

> We understand it in the degree in which we make it a part of our own attitudes, not just by collective information concerning the conditions under which it was produced.... To some degree we become artists ourselves as we undertake this integration, and, by bringing it to pass, our own experience is reoriented.... This insensible melting is far more efficacious than the change effected by reasoning, because it enters directly into attitude.[34]

Yet Dewey was clear that perception involves hard work: "The one who is too lazy, idle, or indurated in convention to perform this work will not see or hear."[35] But when we do, we contribute to making and completing the art because the experience is art.

This idea was taken by artists reading *Art as Experience*. Marcel Duchamp in his 1957 speech "The Creative Act" considered the question of artist and spectator, which he called "the two poles of the creation of art." He concluded:

> All in all, the creative act is not performed by the artist alone; the spectator brings the work in contact with the external world by deciphering and interpreting its inner qualification and thus adds his contribution to the creative act. This becomes even more obvious when posterity gives a final verdict and sometimes rehabilitates forgotten artists.[36]

We hear this thought, too, in Joseph Beuys's mantra: "everyone is an artist."[37] Perhaps more clearly, master meditation teacher Chögyam Trungpa locates the "basic problem in artistic endeavor" as "the tendency to split the artist from the audience and then try to send a message from one to the other. . . . In meditative art, the artist embodies the viewer as well as the creator of the works."[38] This is at the crux of Dewey's proposition to radically shift the role of viewers, giving them agency, seeing them as participants: viewers take part by completing the circle of aesthetic experience, making the work begun by an artist live as *an* experience, integrating it into themselves in meaningful, even transformative ways. In reuniting the artist and audience as cocreators, Dewey reestablished art as useful in coming to consciousness.

Embodied knowing goes beyond mere thinking; it requires full participation. One of the values of contemporary social practice is that it puts us back in touch with that way of knowing, challenging us to pry open our sensibilities and sustain that open state for a time. Then should aesthetic experiences arise and we take them in fully—reflecting on them, consummating them, integrating them into our being—we complete the making of the artwork. It is in such moments that life can also be art. Yet there is a discomfort on the part of critics with the life experiences that are at the core of socially engaged art practice. They favor a tighter approach and seek out feedback from their peers.[39] So we are left with a matter of whose experience matters, of who has greater authority over another. And in this power relationship, art experts award themselves the upper hand. But if we believe, as did Dewey, that art is a valuable way to reflect on one's interior and public life, then the value lies with the one embodying *an* experience.

Dewey's understanding of *an* experience grew from his perceptive aesthetic interest and his embodied way of integrating art into life, living life with an aesthetic awareness of the everyday. For Dewey, reflection is a necessary corollary to having experience; it is how we complete the process and integrate experience as we continue to develop ourselves and realize ways to act more fruitfully in the world. Recognizing that life itself is an accumulation of experiences, Dewey believed the conscious individual uses the past to inform the present and "being fully alive, the future is not ominous but a promise. . . . It consists of possibilities that are felt as a possession of what is now and here. In life that is truly life, everything overlaps and merges." In this, art plays an essential part, for it "celebrates with peculiar intensity the moments in which the past reinforces the present and in which the future is a quickening of what now is."[40]

Dewey believed that it takes time for experience to become *an* experience. "In order to understand the meaning of artistic products, we have to forget them for a time, to turn aside from them and have recourse to the ordinary forces and conditions of experience that we do not usually regard as esthetic."[41] We have to lose them, and then find them again, over time.

Writing of Katie Paterson's *Future Library*, an artwork that uses time as a medium, curator Lisa Le Feuvre considers not just its first hundred years but also the next century when all the commissioned texts will be published, distinguishing experienced time from measured time. She also ponders her own experience of this work, having initially questioned the need to travel to Oslo during winter 2016 to see something that will not be finished until 2114. Her passage was first by plane from England; then, meeting her guide, taking public transit; then trudging through the snow, breathing in the cold clean air, talking all the while; finally reaching a sign in the forest, *Future Library*, where they sat in silence for awhile; then retracing their steps until, back at the start,

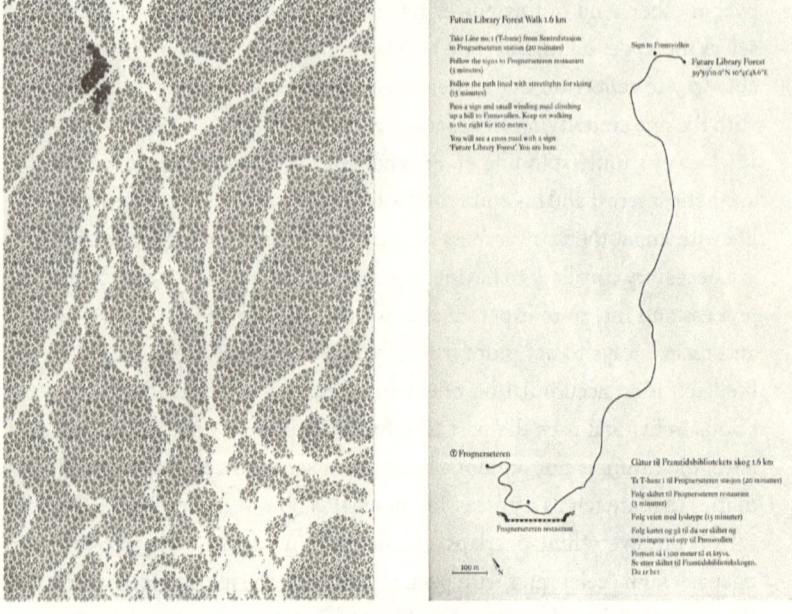

Katie Paterson. *Future Library*, 2014. Two-sided foil block print on paper.
Documentation for project commissioned by Bjørvika Utvikling. Photo:
Courtesy of the artist and Bjørvika Utvikling, Oslo, Norway.

they parted. That was it. But as Le Feuvre writes, "my perception had
changed—my perception of my own time, of the time of an artwork,
and the time of time. There had been no artwork to point to, nothing to
look at, nothing to measure, nothing to chart." She adds: "I like my art
historical facts," but rather here "on this one day I came across a proposal of ideas, an invitation to inhabit something to come. I am still in
the time of *Future Library*."[42]

The process of experiencing comprises manifold moments, as
Dewey understood, and it is different for each person. It also can live on
for a lifetime, even when the work of art is no longer present in front of
us, or no longer even exists as with temporary works, or is over as with
social practice projects, or is not even finished as with *Future Library*.
We experience art not once but again and again as it arises in us. Art becomes part of the ongoing growth processes that are life. And this is true
not only of our experiences with art but is true of all aesthetic experi-

ences, for those with art are but a subset of the wider realm of aesthetic experience essential to being human.

Processing Experience

I think that I didn't truly understand the art experience until I curated the site-specific exhibition *Places with a Past* for the Spoleto Festival USA in Charleston, South Carolina, in 1991. This opportunity came at the right moment; I was a curator suffocating in museums. Working in that small city was more than curating sited works: art was situated within the living history of people. Later, when I thought this chapter of my career had ended,[43] it was reignited into a very different sequel, *Places with a Future.* While a decade prior, artists had sought to make powerful but lesser-known aspects of American history visible through sited installations, the second time around the task was to make the present known. Only now in retrospect can I say that all these efforts were intended for viewers, residents, and visitors to perceive Charleston in a Deweyan aesthetic way: creating greater consciousness, gaining greater agency.

In Charleston it was important for time to pass, for the experiences with art during the first exhibition to settle in before something else could be thoughtfully undertaken, as Dewey said of experience, and for it to be brought to consciousness. It begins with the lived experiences of individuals who had been touched by the works that were on view, those for whom the art, while temporary, continued to live as enduring aesthetic experiences. Such gestation sits outside the art world conventions, with its demands for outcomes at the outset, immediately followed by assessment deadlines once a project is over and the grant report due. Time and again, artists and curators are tasked with setting goals rather than articulating aims at the inception and criticized by writers for what they take to be the endgame.[44] So I have sought a permeable path: not so much an implementation plan as an organic process that can be responsive to the ways artists and publics give themselves to the experience of art, accepting the unknown.[45]

I dare say, there are few places as rich a ground for experience as

Charleston. The city and region encompass a complex way of life, and a people whose conscious, aesthetic way of being embodies the continuity of time of which Dewey spoke.[46] It was there that I experienced how art and the everyday can become intertwined over a lifetime, that is, when art springs from the real. There, committed and invested communities know — as Dewey did — that art takes form not in an exhibition but as an expression of lived culture.

South Carolina in 2000 was a time of protest, with a stormy controversy over flying the Confederate Flag atop the State Capitol building in Columbia. The artists I invited initially were theater director and choreographer Ping Chong, writer Neill Bogan, and photographer and community artist Lonnie Graham, along with assistant curator Tumelo Mosaka, who I first met in his hometown of Johannesburg. Our first moment together, rushing in from the airport, was attending a filled-beyond-capacity theater where residents had gathered to hear southern authors speak about the flag and race.[47]

At that moment I had *an* experience listening to Kendra Hamilton's sultry, melodic voice. At the next annual festival she was in the spotlight again, leading a post-performance discussion of Ping Chong's production of *Secret Histories*, which, unlike those that preceded in his "Undesirable Elements" series, departed from issues of ethnicity to take up questions of black and white. With collaborator Talvin Wilks, Ping Chong interwove the histories of five women whose identities placed them on the edges of society. Sensing the audience's experience might elicit strong reactions, employing this typical educational format became a critical moment of sharing. What I hadn't anticipated was Hamilton's personal experience beyond her role of discussion leader that evening. Six months later she wrote:

> I never got to tell you how I felt. But that experience seems to have completely healed the wounds that I've been carrying around in my heart from growing up in that sick and seductive city since childhood. When I return to Charleston now, to visit my family or do research, it's without that dull ache that used to start throbbing as soon as the pine barrens gave way to the low marshy flats surrounding the city. That is a

gift that you have given. And I only wish there were something I could do to repay you.[48]

She did. Hamilton became an essential member of the emerging *Places with a Future* collaborative, working for much of that decade, along with landscape architect Walter Hood and social choreographer Ernesto Pujol, as we assumed a frequent presence in Charleston, engaging in continuous conversation with citizens.

There were also many projects,[49] but perhaps none so significant as working with the Phillips Community. Located twenty-five miles outside of Charleston, this enclave of six hundred residents is made up of descendants of African and African American freed men, middle-class tradesmen, and businessmen who bought land in ten-acre tracts for $63 around 1878 under the US Freedmen's Bureau. Knowing that their ancestors had no land rights previous to that time, many being property themselves, those residents held that trust sacred. For all intents and purposes, Phillips had always been the proverbial "place out in the middle of nowhere," lacking the usual codes by which historic significance is demarcated (such as great houses or great oaks) and so perceived as a place of little value going forward. But as the paved roads, fences, and gated entries of nearby housing developments became inscribed on the land, Phillips was for the first time becoming legible and its low-lying bottomland, once forgotten land, sought after.

Community Association President Richard Habersham took part in a conversation staged by Suzanne Lacy and Rick Lowe in 2003, and had returned the next year as part of a program on the subject of gentrification. He was compelling as he spoke of anticipated changes to their legacy land and what would be lost. The elders he represented believed the solution was building a community center to both nurture their youth and ground their claim. Habersham's passion and clarity of mission, along with his openness to artists whose work resonated with his community's issues, was inspiring to us. Then with patience and grace, he showed willingness to inhabit the unknown with us as we pursued an open path of creative inquiry over the next five years.

To listen deeply is to unearth the values by which life is lived. These values deepen more still during an iterative process as participants grow to occupy a safe space and think out loud together—something Ernesto Pujol was especially adept at cultivating among the group as he urged sustaining open minds. To be in such a challenging process is to be fully conscious. Sometimes, it is just sitting together with a shared "not-knowingness." Yet occupying this unrestricted, in-between space of becoming is essential for real growth to occur, Dewey knew. The goal cannot be predetermined; it needs to arise slowly over time. My role as curator was to curate the process: holding open the space for collaboration and a possible meeting of minds, for new ideas to emerge and right ways to be revealed.[50]

At a certain point, it was curatorially necessary to widen the space even further and shift perceptual positions. So the artistic team sought a mechanism by which long-time residents—insiders—could benefit from the perspective we had gained as outsiders, allowing them to see their place through fresh eyes, make new connections, see themselves as part of a greater whole. Getting out of your place and out of yourself in body and mind, using your imagination to conjure new images, if only for a time, has deep value because it is in those moments when consciousness expands and potentiality arises.

It was Kendra Hamilton again who suggested we visit African-American communities historically tied to their land. She plotted an itinerary that took us by bus to Sapelo Island and Harris Neck in Georgia, communities forced to succumb to change and loss of property; and to American Beach and Eatonville in Florida, which had evolved and survived. Traveling together, artists and Phillips citizens, outsiders alike, afforded critical ways of considering old problems, and we headed back to Phillips with what Buddhists call a beginner's mind to start anew.

To shift the way you look at place also demands changing how you name it. This led to Walter Hood's notion of *lifeways*. He wrote: "The nomenclature of things is powerful in our society and culture. It has more power than the thing itself. . . . Changing the nomenclature from community design to community lifeways makes it possible to think more about the way of life in communities. Paying attention to lifeways suggests that focusing on the *way* people live in a place yields different project results, as opposed to thinking about how designers want people to live in a place."[51]

In the end our work as a creative team did not result in a community center in Phillips. There had never been a funding mandate to do so, though a grant was secured to purchase communal land for this purpose. But importantly during those years of dialogue, what did come about was the recognition that the way of life in Phillips *is* sustainable because the lifeways of its citizens are in accordance with the land. To see this was all a matter of perception and to appreciate it, was to share in the values of this community. Phillips residents use only what they need, leaving the rest to serve as habitat for wildlife and a safe migratory route for birds. They have not extensively paved their community, do not possess motorboats, and because they do not have golf courses as in nearby gated developments, they do not produce runoff, thus polluting the creek or the ground as others do in the surrounding newer developments. They live in harmony with rather than overtake nature. Theirs is a community of cooperative land management, offering a model for a sustainable future from which other communities can learn.

Our work had another result. It ignited an idea for Michael Allen, a National Park Service Ranger with whom we often consulted. He was inspired by the artists' projects and more so their processes, leading him to make connections beyond this small, localized place and to see it as part of a greater whole. Seeking to bring to a conscious level the way history is present in the geography of the region, he urged the writing and passage of the Gullah/Geechee Cultural Heritage Corridor Act by the US Congress: legislation which recognizes and preserves the unique contributions of captive Africans along the Atlantic coast from North Carolina to Florida.[52] This bold plan was of a scale and ambition far grander than any curatorial or artistic program we could have imagined, and, fittingly, it came about by another route, through the primary aesthetic experience of life.

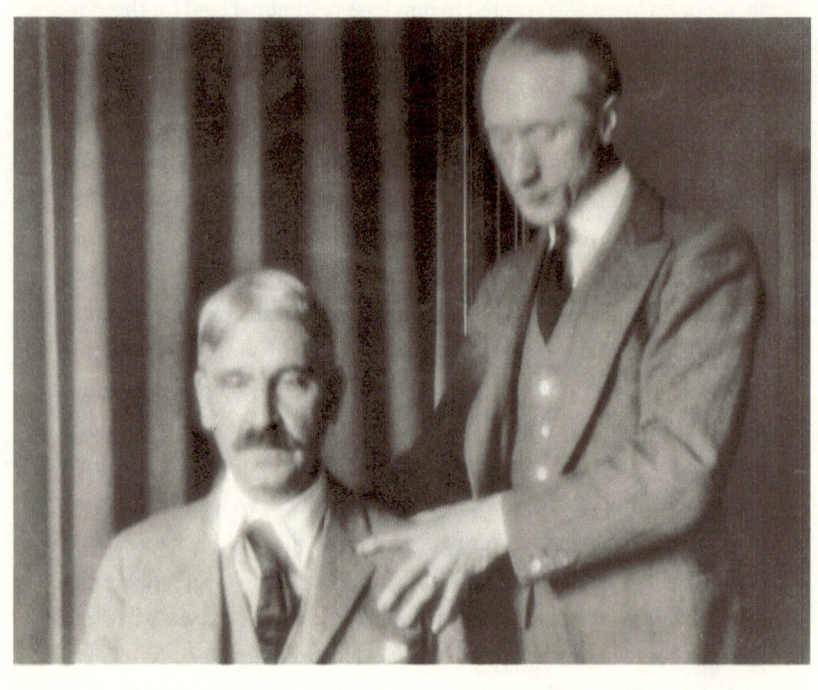

John Dewey and F. M. Alexander, c. 1918. Special Collections Research Center,
Morris Library, Southern Illinois University, Carbondale.

3 Practice

When living is a practice, life is an ever-evolving work of art. Historically, artists had a medium, a subject, and a style. Currently, many artists speak of having a *practice*. I welcome that term. Doctors and lawyers refer to their work as a practice, indicating the totality and credibility of what they do. Artists are often deemed (and demeaned) as free and inspired yet reckless spirits, not regarded as equals to the professional class in their craft. The combined term *art practice* verifies their training and the seriousness of their enterprise. Like *style, practice* is also a verb, yet it conveys a deeper way of making. We practice to get better at something, to perfect what we do. It is not a technique we get right and then repeat by habit; rather, as Dewey advocated, we are consciously present, so that each instance is lived anew. Over time we develop and change, which the philosopher saw as a necessary way of being in a constantly changing environment. Thus, as life unfolds, we remain in a continual state of becoming.

Artists and curators, in fact all of us, not only need *to* practice, but to cultivate *a* practice over a lifetime. To Dewey, to have a practice also gives form to our beliefs and, as we embody them, communicates our values to others as we put them into practice. So as a life path for artists, or anyone doing what they do as an art, practice goes to the core of their being.

A practice is not synonymous with a profession; it is more than that. We sense this in the question of architect Toyo Ito, as he struggled to address Japan's devastation wrought by the 2011 earthquake and tsunami: "I instinctively felt that I had to contemplate the essential question of 'What is architecture?' all over again."[1] Now Ito knows what architecture is and how to make it, yet in the Kamaishi revival project he was not operating as the principal of his Tokyo-based architectural practice. This situation, where nearly everything was leveled and so many died, demanded that he work differently, so he joined a five-member architectural team. But even more so, he found he had to access the very root of his practice, to live it in a reinvigorated way, abandoning master planning and working directly with residents to enable them to imagine their future. He wrote of this experience: "Pursuing architecture in this way — in its purest form, which is from the heart — was an amazing thing and made me feel as if I would require no more training for my future career."[2]

No more master plans. This organic approach recalls the permeable processes of the *Places with a Future* team — with Kendra Hamilton, Walter Hood, and Ernesto Pujol — that led to the revelation of lifeways in the Phillips Community. There, rather than implementing a plan, we chose to embody a deep listening process through which the values of the community could rise and, being heard, could be traced in the landscape. Later, Hood would call it a "speculative practice." This dynamic, emergent way of working, indebted to artists' practices to which Hood became exposed, was different from the professional practices of architecture and landscape design that he knew in which the outcome must be predefined. Speculative practice allows for uniquely appropriate answers to evolve that respect how people live in a place, their relationships to the environment, and their cultural histories. But one has to trust the process, and it must be lived as Pujol described: "To be thinking-making at all times, not a job-related making but an uninterrupted critical creative state, so that we walk through society in and with this state of non-art making, looking at life. Making brings us back to the senses, sensations, and experiences. To be in a state of practice, being outside the studio, generates more experiences. It is a practice state."[3] Dewey recognized that when making happens in this way and we trust the process, knowledge expands in unexpected, fruitful ways.

Dewey's Practice

Dewey had an embodied practice. From his late fifties to early eighties, he trained with master practitioner Frederick Matthias Alexander in a mode of conscious control designed to promote awareness of posture and breathing. Dewey credited the Alexander Technique for his improved health and longevity, but it was more than a device to relieve the aging philosopher's aches and pains. It impacted his ideas and played a role in his writing from 1916 onward.[4] Yet to really understand what this practice meant, he said, one has to enact it. "I don't talk about it very much because unless one has had personal experience, it sounds to others just like another one of those enthusiasms for some pet panacea."[5]

The challenge lay, as Dewey saw it, in that we become immune to the very things closest to us, including the capabilities we possess. We need to redirect dulling habits and undergo a "reeducation" of perception. Recognizing that this eludes common conception, we need a "concrete procedure," and "this indispensable thing is exactly what Mr. Alexander has accomplished."[6] Moreover, practice was socially imperative:

> Clearly we have not carried the plane of conscious control, the direction of action by perception of connections, far enough. We cannot separate organic life and mind from physical nature without also separating nature from life and mind. The separation has reached a point where intelligent persons are asking whether the end is to be a catastrophe, the subjection of man to the industrial and military machines he has created. This situation confers peculiar poignancy upon the fact that just where connections and interdependencies are most numerous, intimate and pervasive, in living, psycho-physical activity, we most ignore unity and connection, and trust most unreservedly in our deliberate beliefs to the isolated and specific — which signifies that in

action we commit ourselves to the unconscious and subconscious, to blind instinct and impulse and routine, disguised and rationalized by all sorts of honorific titles. Thus we are brought to the topic of consciousness.[7]

But if individuals acted in an integrated way, in accordance with the natural functions of the human organism, society itself would function better. For this, we must understand the continuity of mind and body — and that was just what Alexander's method demonstrated. Dewey went to great lengths to verify that his claim was tested and scientific. Impassioned, he pleaded his case to the New York Academy of Medicine in 1928, saying that division is "so deep-seated that it has affected even our language. We have no word by which to name mind-body in a unified wholeness of operation.... Consequently, when we discuss the matter, when we talk of the relations of mind *and* body and endeavor to establish their unity in human conduct, we still speak of body *and* mind, unconsciously perpetuating the very division we are striving to deny.... What the facts testify to is not an influence exercised across and between two separate things, but to behavior so integrated that it is artificial to split it up into two things."[8]

Yet to practice mind-body unity was challenging. Dewey shared, "I had the most humiliating experience of my life, intellectually speaking," as he began to learn the Alexander Technique and was unable to follow directions to do "such a seemingly simple act as to sit down." He had to develop a practice. Finding insufficient "all the mental capacity which one prides [oneself] upon possessing," Dewey found this "not an experience congenial to one's vanity."[9] Instead he had to let go and learn to trust the process. And he looked to historical precedents, citing for instance Confucianism:

> ... the idea of non-doing can hardly be stated and explained; it can only be felt. It is something more than mere inactivity; it is a kind of rule of moral doing, a doctrine of active patience, endurance, persistence while nature has time to do her work. Conquering by yielding is its motto.... The Chinese philosophy of life embodies a profoundly

valuable contribution to human culture and one of which a hurried, impatient, over-busied and anxious West is infinitely in need.[10]

When visiting Japan in 1919, Dewey also found living evidence in the art of judo. He wrote home to his daughters:

> . . . I think it is much better than most of our inside formal gymnastics. The mental element is much stronger. In short, I think a study ought to be made here from the standpoint of conscious control. Tell Mr. Alexander to get a book by Harrison — compatriot of his — out of the library, called "The Fighting Spirit of Japan." It is a journalist's book, not meant to be deep, but is interesting and said to be reliable as far as it goes. I noticed at the Judo the small waists of those people; they breathe always from the abdomen . . . I have yet to see a Japanese throw his head back when he rises.[11]

This was a body error that the Alexander Technique sought to correct, that is, we lead with our heads, hence strain our necks when we get up.

Art Practice

Dewey had another life practice and that was looking at art. To practice the arts of living, as he called them, is "a matter of communication and participation in values of life by means of the imagination, and works of art are the most intimate and energetic means of aiding individuals to share in the arts of living."[12] Art aids us in the practice of life, as we develop the habit of fully breathing in experience, making meaning that is integral to our sense of being; then, breathing it out as we act more consciously in the world, with an understanding of the consequences of our actions in relation to others and to the planet.

The poetry of the everyday, what Dewey saw as aesthetic experience in a life lived artfully, can be cultivated and put into practice through our experiences with works of art. "When the liberating of human capacity operates as a socially creative force," the philosopher wrote, "art will not be a luxury, a stranger to the daily occupations of making a living.

Making a living economically speaking, will be at one with making a life that is worth living."[13] Although the function of art eluded his contemporaries, Dewey staunchly believed that experiencing works of art had a useful role in the living of life. Thus, he wrote in 1925:

> The present confusion, deemed chaos by some, in the fine arts and esthetic criticism seems to be an inevitable consequence of the underlying, even if unavowed, separation of the instrumental and the consummatory.... For these critics, in proclaiming that esthetic qualities in works of fine art are unique, in asserting their separation from not only every thing that is existential in nature but also from all other forms of good, in proclaiming that such arts as music, poetry, painting have characters unshared with any natural things whatsoever:
> —in asserting such things the critics carry to its conclusion the isolation of fine art from the useful, of the final from efficacious. They thus prove that the separation of the consummation from the instrumental makes art wholly esoteric.[14]

Dewey found allies among modern artists. The year after he published *Art as Experience*, artist-educator Josef Albers echoed the depth of Dewey's concept of pursuing *an* experience of life as art, writing: "artistic seeing and artistic living are a deeper seeing and living." He added that at Black Mountain College, where he was in residence at that time, they seek students who see "that real art is essential life and essential life is art."[15] At the suggestion of the college's rector, John Andrew Rice, Albers titled his article "Art as Experience." Dewey's ideas had already greatly influenced Rice in founding this educational experiment— a pedagogical testing ground for the unity of mind and body, where art and life were one. One Black Mountain student, Robert Rauschenberg, later famously spoke of acting in the gap between art and life,[16] yet for Dewey, there is no gap when we live life as a conscious experience.

Wolfgang Laib is an artist who lives his life as art. He studied medicine but never went into medical practice, instead cultivating a conscious way of making art and being in the world. His art practice is one with his life practice. Laib offers that to others, too, as he seeks to create

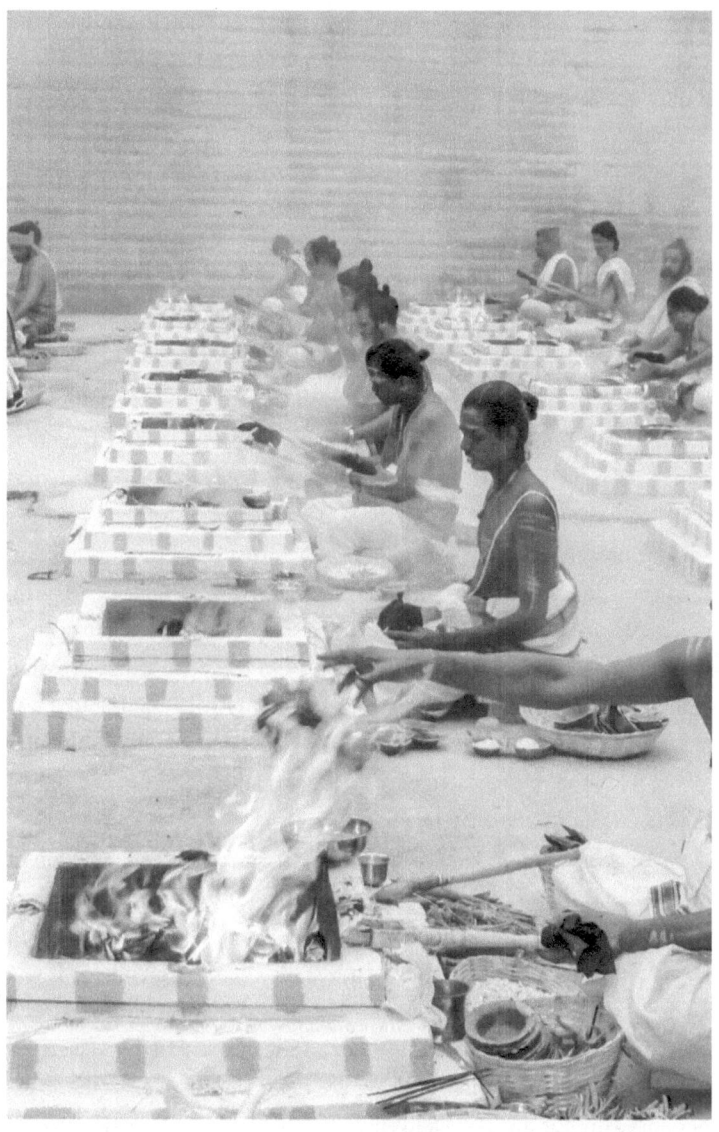

Wolfgang Laib. *Mahayagna*, 2009. Forty-five Brahmin priests officiate the fire ritual at the Fondazione Merz, Turin, Italy. Photo: Claudio Cravero, courtesy the artist and Sperone Westwater, New York.

a living art, perpetuating a "sense of life . . . to keep something alive" and engaging the viewer directly.[17] Take his 2009 project at the Merz Foundation in Turin, Italy. It began as an intensely focused conversation with Brahmins in Tamil Nadu, the state in southern India where he and his wife Carolyn spend part of each year; his intention was to keep alive the work of Mario Merz, an artist with whom he had a close relationship. As Carolyn further elucidates the resulting project, "it was for us like a mutual act of prayer. Being a little bit shy of that word, it was a gesture different kinds of people were making at the same moment, so that the energy of all beings in that space in that time were relevant to what was happening. In that sense, it had its own life beyond our preparations, beyond what the Brahmins were trying to achieve. . . . Everything that happened had to do with all the living energy that was found at that moment. . . . It was to create a life-giving moment."

For his father's eightieth birthday, the artist drew upon the Tamil Nadu custom of visualizing the number of full moons since one's birth, placing 1,008 rice mountains in the open space of the sparely furnished home they share in southern Germany. "So often we think of being eighty, as 'I'm getting old, approaching death,'" Carolyn said, "but it was the opposite. There was a richness shared by everybody." This is the life-giving force that Dewey sought to convey when he spoke of the vitalizing effect of aesthetic experience.

Wolfgang often says that "the difference between yellow pigment and pollen is the whole story of life," Carolyn further shares. "You have to be one with the work—look at it, smell it, think about it. You have to receive it; you have to be receptive to the life energy in an object. If you do that repeatedly over long periods of time, if that is your practice, it becomes an acute kind of existence or a state of mind that you learn."[18] In Dewey's understanding of living life as an art practice, aesthetic experiences do not just have a liveliness, they have an energetic sense of aliveness. That is what Wolfgang Laib manifests through the care he puts into making and what Katie Paterson imagines in the forest.

Process as Practice

In his day, Dewey bemoaned that the creative aspect of attaining happiness was being flattened into something that could be purchased, a pleasure commodity:

> Such a point of view treats concrete activities and specific interests not as worth while [sic] in themselves, or as constituents of happiness, but as mere external means to getting pleasures.... [Then] art, poetry, religion and the state [became] mere servile means of attaining sensuous enjoyments. Since pleasure was an outcome, a result valuable on its own account independently of the active processes that went into it, happiness was a thing to be possessed and held onto. The acquisitive instincts of man were exaggerated at the expense of the creative. Production was of importance not because of the intrinsic worth of invention and reshaping the world, but because its external results feed pleasure ... making the end passive and possessive.... Material comfort and ease were magnified in contrast with the pains and risk of experimental creation.[19]

American urban studies theorist Richard Florida once drew admiration from city officials and developers for advocating art and cultural experiences in the course of daily life, promoting the "Creative Class lifestyle" as "a passionate quest for experience." He looked to stimulation provided by "indigenous street-level culture—a teeming blend of cafes, sidewalk musicians, and small galleries and bistros, where it is hard to draw the line between participant and observer, or between creativity and its creators."[20] Florida's ideas and corollary statistics favored gentrification developments that cared little for existing evidence of lived culture—lifeways—instead adopting bits of it in ersatz replicas, for instance, as decorative motifs in trendy restaurants with the flavor of the uprooted past but without the lived experience.

This is a far cry from Dewey's (and later, Pirsig's) distinction between being a spectator or a participant in one's own life, and from Dewey's promotion (and subsequently, Beuys's) of the creative capacity of all individuals. Somewhere along the way, values changed, and Dewey's philosophy of art-as-experience was repurposed so that to be a participant meant the pleasure and immediate gratification of being a consumer. But if worth is solely sited in diversionary enjoyments, then gone is the challenge that we are brought to through aesthetic experiences to make change in ourselves and society. And while Florida's notion of community is a feedback loop of perpetually expanding commerce, for Dewey community is steeped in communication and cooperation, with an eye to the common good. It is about relationship making, not place making. Unlike Florida's world, in which things — and experiences — exist in a continual consumption cycle of purchase and depletion, experiences for Dewey are an inexhaustible resource: as we breathe in and out experiences of art or in life, they are replenished with more experiences generously generated for us and for others. This, to Dewey, was what living life was all about.

Ernesto Pujol finds that "art as social practice bears the original purpose of art at its core: the evolution of human consciousness."[21] Dewey would agree. Yet troublingly, he finds these projects are often "tied to American materialism in terms of collective entitlement to abundance. Some projects are not seeking individual and collective consciousness, but merely the redistribution of material wealth." He continued:

> Historically, we have witnessed the best the human spirit could offer in its desire to transcend material life. But during the twentieth century, the visual arts, which had been one of the main components of culture for hundreds of years, were imperceptibly divorced from cultural production right under our noses, slowly turned into urban commodities disconnected from Nature and populist usefulness, increasingly invested in the erasure of memory and the promotion of materialism as the hallmarks of modernity. This separation extricated the human spirit's transcendent cultural component, so all that has remained is an urban elite product based on talent, skills, esthetics, theoretical arguments, and speculative market value that regards most pre-capitalism cultural production as intellectually suspect and sentimental.[22]

Pujol seeks to put the visual arts back into the culture-at-large, still preserving the true meaning of consciousness, mindfulness, and intention that have been absorbed into today's lifestyle and artspeak. So in 2015, he undertook a continuous three-day performance entitled 9–5. Sited in a Wall Street office tower, he went to the source to enact "the economy of consciousness rather than of capital, or perhaps," as he wrote, "a different capital: the wealth of deep presence."

When process is a practice, it requires our full presence. Pujol calls it "vulnerability as methodology."[23] It starts with the beginner's mind of "don't know":[24] the state of conscious unknowingness, where preconceptions (to Buddhists) or habits or mere recognition (to Dewey) are set aside so that we might see what we never recognized, or re-recognize what we have come to no longer see or feel within the all-too-familiar present. It is a state of openness. Dewey believed this was a requirement for every true experimental process, of which an artist's creative process was his supreme example. The open mind is the generative place from which potentiality springs. But this is no easy feat—it only comes with practice—because opening the mind to see more clearly, to see something new or anew, is to engage the question with our whole being.

From an embodied point of view, we feel an experience before fully absorbing it into our consciousness. So the creative mind needs to be open to the workings of intuition, which are often denied as a true source of knowledge. Yet intuition is a direct link to the unconscious, to muscle memory, not just the brain but the mind-body unity of which Dewey spoke. Intuition springs from a wholeness. And Dewey knew intuition is a way of knowing that exists within all of us. "What is the landscape of permission you have to put around yourself to move from knowing to not knowing?" queries Ann Hamilton.[25] Recognizing intuition as a way of knowing from deep inside gives us that permission. So we need to locate it and trust it.

This process can be uncomfortable, triggering a state of uncertainty that runs counter to our natural human desire for security, Dewey admonished. The creative phase is filled with doubt and passes through a "disturbed, troubled, ambiguous, confused"[26] state, he wrote. Yet he observed that these chaotic periods are essential: "Life grows when a

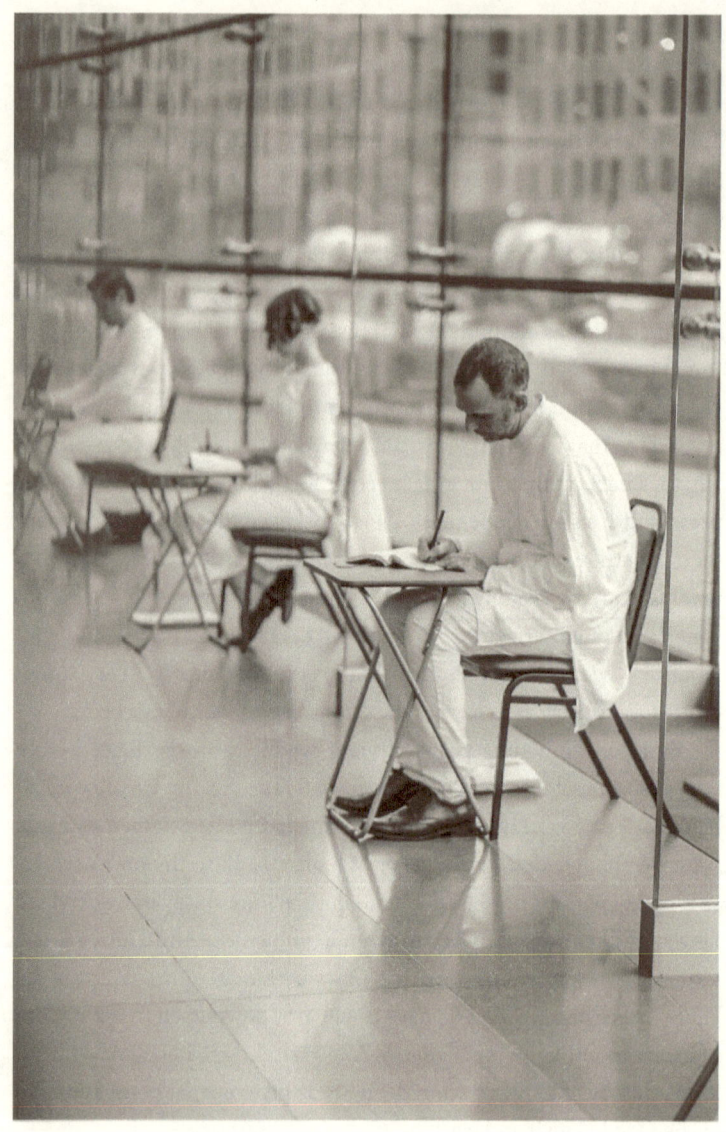

Ernesto Pujol. 9–5, 2015. Brookfield Place Pavilion, Lower Manhattan, New York.
Photo: Nisa Ojalvo, courtesy More Art, New York.

temporary falling out is a transition to a more extensive balance of the energies of the organism with those of the conditions under which it lives."[27] So, it is important that periods of intense striving are sustained, and Dewey thought artists are especially good at that. But practice is required.

In this process, whether in life or art, it is critical to have clarity of intent or, as Dewey said of all thinking, the "condition of our having aims."[28] Goals come later. To set goals before the exploration nullifies the experimental nature of inquiry, and then we set off on the wrong track.[29] Instead, aims derive from articulating the right questions. Aims steer the course and guide us. They drive us with a sense of why the inquiry matters, now. Rooted in our values, aims act as barometers, so we can weather ambiguity and transcend obstacles, using knowledge that comes through research and planning as well as accidentally, all the while maintaining openness to what the process might reveal when we live it.

Dewey sought to analyze how the process of inquiry is carried out as an embodied creative continuum, identifying four stages: dialectical, relational, progressive, and continual. The dialectical stage moves between doing or trying and reflecting. The relational occurs when connections are made. In the progressive: "Each step forward, each 'means' used, is a partial attainment of an 'end.' It makes clearer the character of that end, and hence suggests to an observing mind the next step to be taken, or the means and methods to be next employed."[30] But Dewey was quick to add: "While a conclusion follows from antecedents, it does not follow from 'premises,' in the strict, formal sense."[31] Hence the process of creative inquiry is not linear, and it is also continual, so that the "time of consummation is also one of beginning anew" as a new process starts.[32]

The concept of means-ends continuum became a cornerstone in Dewey's philosophy. The end of a creative process was not a "terminal point, external to the conditions that have led up to it"; rather, the end was "the continually developing meaning of present tendencies." Then, ends become the means of propelling next stages within a sustained continuity of creativity and change. Moreover, in the continual flow of creative process enacted, embodied, and lived, "the process is art and its product, no matter at what stage it be taken, is a work of art."[33]

This is critical to an understanding of the process and ontological state (the product) of socially engaged art practice, which often delivers a creative process instead of a traditional art product as it employs life processes as an art medium. It has also become the basis for many an argument in this field. But if the process of life is ultimately "a work of art," as Dewey said, then there is no need to demand any other aesthetic result than life itself.[34] Additionally, the more artists launch processes (rather than author things), the more they succeed in creating art as experiences. Thus, a project's effect can be measured by its integration among the persons whose experiences become fuller as they are lived. Furthermore, with the dissipation of the traditional boundaries of art's object-ness, the social bond experienced by communities, transitory or enduring, lives on as we grow and change.

In the process, social practice creates a changed reality for a place, for a person, and for a people. That is its art and it is ongoing. The "end is no longer a terminus or limit to be reached. It is the active process of transforming the existent situation. Not perfection as a final goal, but the ever-enduring process of perfecting, maturing, refining is the aim in living."[35] When we practice, we live and work within this creative continuum. One creative gesture opens the way for the next unendingly.

Cultivating a Life Practice

A condition of modern life is the perception that time and space are shrinking around us. Dewey experienced this throughout his own life. To reclaim a fuller experience of time and space has been one of the attractions of Buddhist mindfulness since its introduction to the US in the late nineteenth century; in the following decades it was adopted by many artists striving for deeper insight through their practice. It takes time to bring to consciousness one's imaginings and to trust one's intuitions, to inhabit the "empty space" that Buddhists say is not empty but full of potential. So the task becomes how to stay creative, thus, fully conscious.

One way is having a creative practice that has a sustainable rhythm, a recurring return to a generative inquiry, so that ideas can surface and flow, and results be realized. So many artists have sought meditation to further their creative practices. For Eugen Herrigel, focus achieved through meditative breathing was the way to perfect the practice of shooting an arrow. His problem was not that he had not practiced enough, but that he did not have a practice. At first, breathing was the focus, but later he wrote: "I learned to lose myself so effortlessly in the breathing that I sometimes had the feeling that I myself was not breathing but — strange as this may sound — being breathed." "Out of the fullness of this presence of mind, disturbed by no clear ulterior motive, the artist who is released from all attachment must practice his art," and "before ever he begins to devote and adjust himself to his task, the artist summons forth this presence of mind and makes sure of it through practice."[36] F. M. Alexander expressed the same when he said it was "not in the movement or standing but in the readiness to stand."[37] I see this in curating, with a readiness in attending to others' processes, solo and collective, so that they can flow and unfold; to taking care so that even seemingly incidental occurrences or ideas tentatively ventured come back to contribute should the time prove right — caring for the process both in the making and in the eventual product seen, read, heard, or felt. While it may at times appear to be "organizing," this way of curating is to have process as a practice.[38]

For Katie Paterson, consistent and productive tasks are meditative practices by which she finds we can "feel our orbit." With greater awareness achieved through Zen-like activities, she arrives at moments of heightened vitality, while also experiencing "breathing as a time-keeper of life." And she knows when this is lacking, "ideas are not released, I don't feel good."[39] She senses being out of balance with the universe. But when ideas come naturally and flow quickly, it feels freeing, and with this freedom comes a feeling of vitality. Therefore, she seeks to become attuned to the seasons, to access the landscape and follow its rhythms, and to cultivate a life art practice.

As Dewey knew, the growth we experience with greater consciousness affirms our aliveness. And Paterson shares: "I feel the most alive when making the most of my whole mind and body, accessing all my capabilities, seeing things more clearly. This is creative, what it is to create, and grow."[40] However, this is not just her remedy but one multiplied through endless examples of artists over time. And not just artists. It is what Jeon's father experienced on the mountaintop. As Dewey intuited and then reasoned, it is the fully human way of being. The challenge is to make it last a lifetime—to become a life practice.

Finally, an opening up, a wider sense of time and space in life, is what artists offer to audiences through the experience of their art. Chögyam Trungpa writes that the art of meditative experience "is a perpetually growing process in which we begin to appreciate our surroundings in life, whatever they may be—it doesn't necessarily have to be good, beautiful, and pleasurable at all. The definition of art, from his point of view, is to be able to see the uniqueness of everyday experience." This "art in everyday life" is enacted as we bring this way of being an artist into everything we do.[41] And this is the practice many seek to find for themselves in the experience that is art.

PART TWO

The Social Value of Art

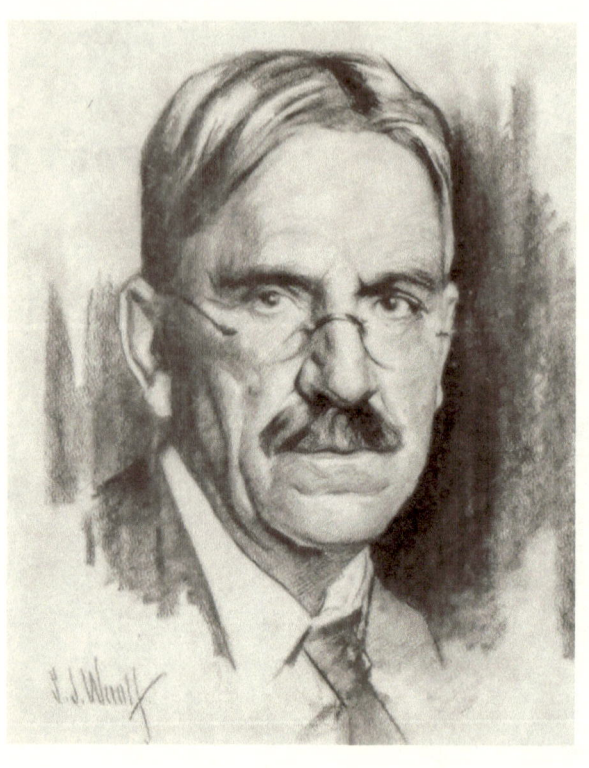

John Dewey, cover of *Time* (detail), June 4, 1928.

4   Democracy

In 1937 Dewey published his essay "Democracy Is Radical." The title was no hyperbole. The recent appropriation of the term "democracy" by the Nazi Party had urged him on, yet he admitted we Americans had also done some considerable distorting of the concept. "There is something to be said for the assertion that the so-called democratic states of the world have achieved only 'bourgeois' democracy . . . one in which power rests finally in the hands of finance capitalism, no matter what claims are made for government of, by and for all the people." So Dewey advised reinvesting in democracy, stating there is "nothing more radical than insistence upon democratic methods as the means by which radical social changes be effected."[1]

In his pamphlet "Against Competition," Marc Fischer makes a case for cooperation over the competition that permeates every aspect of the art world, describing it as "a treadmill made from decomposing shit that is so devoid of nutrients that even its compost won't allow anything fresh to grow. We need something better to run on," he says. Advocating against capitalist-inspired concepts such as marketing art as new and improved or perpetually seeking the new trend or "turn," Fischer looks to the value the past can offer. "This older soil remains fertile for new plantings."[2] It's no wonder that Temporary Services, founded by Fischer and Brett Bloom in 1998, have also started Half Letter Press to spread the word and give visibility to the ideas and ethics of those creative individuals they deem productive in making a more democratic culture.

Temporary Services' tactics recycle and extend strategies begun in the 1970s when the contemporary art world in the US (with a new infusion of NEA money) sought again to widen the art system as during the WPA. This time it took on a campaign to dismantle the postwar art world myth that had put painting by white males at the pinnacle of a hierarchy dominated by New York galleries and museums, with collectors' purchases becoming investments with a high return on the dollar. Artists punched holes in that structure when they started independent, alternative spaces across the country to actively support the work of emerging and underrepresented artists. Meanwhile performance art, artists' books, mail art, video, and other media defied the art market by being ephemeral, mass-produced, or free, leaving critics at sea to identify the next "-ism" during what they called the pluralist decade.

By the mid-eighties, artists' groups came to the forefront to collectively confront inequities in art and politics—Border Art Workshop/Taller de Arte Fronterizo in 1984, Guerrilla Girls in 1985, Act Up in 1987, and others—giving grist to the question of who the artist is. Working together was critical to taking social action, and by the 1990s artists teaming up with public constituencies caused even greater critical consternation as collaboration for a cause propelled social practice into the new century. Along with these do-it-yourself efforts, open source and the gift economy demonstrated that art and capitalism do not necessarily go hand in hand. These decades also saw a rehabilitation of regionalism with New Museum founder Marcia Tucker championing "art outside the mainstream," later reinvented as a globalist outlook in a decentered art world.

Yet the pull and power of the mainstream art world is formidable. Daniel J. Martinez says: "I for one am grateful for all the different types of artists there are; isn't that the point of a culture—to contain the widest range of points of view and of artistic production. The rub is that there is a perception that all artists seek the same goals. Success does not have a singular definition. Some want money, others fame, some you never know what they want."[3] Today there is an ever more powerful mainstream with its museum-scale commercial galleries, museums as big business, auctions, and art fairs in which the hot artist of the moment signals the survival of the fittest. And therein lies the problem for Dewey.

Western individualism, which by now has spread to every corner of the world, was in Dewey's time the necessary means for modern success, a concept synonymous with economic prosperity. In America, individualism — based on initiative, vigor, and independence — "assumed a romantic form . . . which equated personal gain with social advance."[4] As Dewey saw it, this perception in the US led to an "enormous exaggeration of material and materialistic economics that now prevails at the expense of cultural values."[5] "For me," counters Martinez, "success is the opportunity to go beyond who and what I am as an artist today, looking forward to the unknown."[6]

Can initiative, vigor, and independence also promote personal growth and social evolution in keeping with democratic values? Can they serve individual and collective needs at once? "I had to unlearn all that society had expected from me," remarked Tania Bruguera, disentangling success from money, respectability from institutions, "in order to be able to learn what I expected of myself." What ultimately proved important to her was to know why she was doing her work. Now she advises young artists to do their work "under any circumstance and to be inspired by every circumstance," and to do "what is good for your art, even when it is not good for your career." For Bruguera this also means you must "find your community, sometimes . . . build your community. . . . to have an inspired and creative dialogue with someone for years."[7]

Marc Fischer makes the case for how and why artists should build networks around shared interests and values: "When artists work with others, they complicate their practice and these collaborations often enrich everything they do. . . . In the process, they learn to write, organize, publish, curate, educate and do anything else necessary to bolster support and dialogue for the ideas they value. More than anything, they learn to take the initiative and build something larger than themselves."[8] Dewey put it this way: "What is learned and employed in an occupation having an aim and involving cooperation with others is moral knowl-

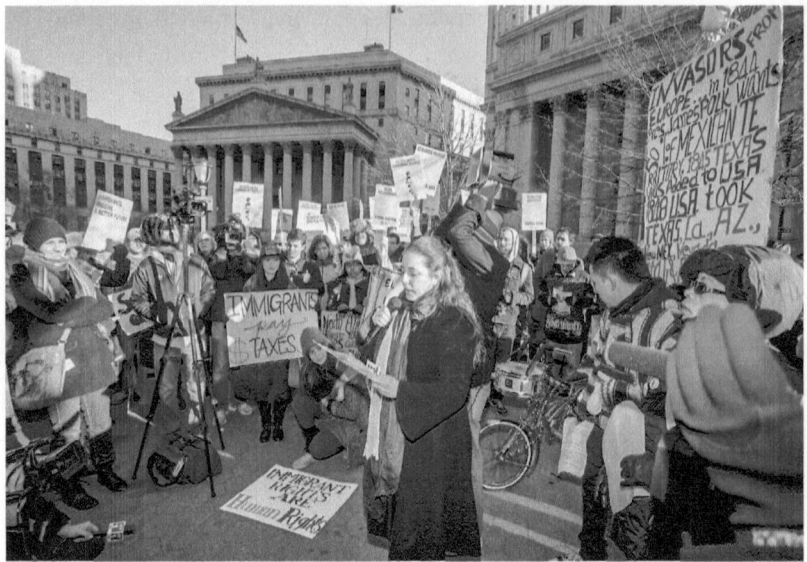

Tania Bruguera. Immigrant Movement International, 2013. Photo: Sam Horine, courtesy Creative Time, New York.

edge, whether consciously so regarded or not. For it builds up a social interest and confers the intelligence needed to make that interest effective in practice."[9]

Constant Change and Enduring Values

For John Dewey—with one foot in nineteenth-century evolutionism and the other in twentieth-century physics—change was a fact of life in the modern world. The real is the material of change. He believed the experimental method allowed us to learn from experience, so that "the test of knowledge became the ability to bring about certain changes."[10] In past eras, "change has been feared. It had been looked upon as the source of decay and degeneration . . . the cause of disorder, chaos, and anarchy," so fixity came to characterize religion, politics, science, and philosophy because "the permanent was the sole ground of assurance and support amid the vicissitudes of existence."[11] But modern science proved differently. With Einstein's theory of relativity and Heisenberg's uncertainty principle, the intellectual community's understanding of the laws to which we are subject needed to catch up. The times demanded it. In 1929, on the eve of the Great Depression, the philosopher prophetically wrote *The Quest for Certainty: A Study of the Relation of Knowledge and Action.*

Although change is a constant, how we engage it determines the future. Dewey pointed out that the modern mind had "confused rapidity of change with advance, and we took certain gains in our own comfort and ease as signs that cosmic forces were working inevitably to improve the whole state of human affairs."[12] Instead Dewey called for the "commitment of liberalism to experimental procedure [which] carries with it the idea of continuous reconstruction of the ideas of individuality and of liberty, in their intimate connection with changes in social relations."[13] So he reasoned, "this rapid change of conditions affords an *opportunity* for progress, but is not itself progress."[14] Progress "depends not on the existence of social change but on the direction which human beings deliberately give that change. . . . It depends upon human intent and aim and upon acceptance of responsibility for its production."[15]

Barely two months into World War II, in his address "Creative Democracy—The Task Before Us," Dewey laid out the challenge each generation faces in a changing world: to give life to the values by which we live and re-create them, because democracy is a living thing, a lived practice. As a creative process, it must respond to the circumstances of our time. Most of all, as a creative act, democracy is perpetually unfinished, always in-progress.

The art of democracy—for it is a creative way of life we make and keep making—is driven by what we care about. Social institutions had to continue to extend rights and keep freedom alive. And while citizens grew in individual agency, they needed to remain responsible to democratic values and create a caring culture. Democracy is not "based upon the traditional ideas which make the individual and the state readymade entities in themselves," but rather democracy "is but a name for the fact that human nature is developed only when its elements take part in directing things which are common, things for the sake of which men and women form groups—families, industrial companies, governments, churches, scientific associations and so on."[16] In this task, democracy stood apart: "Every other form of moral and social faith rests upon the idea that experience must be subjected at some point or other to some form of external control; to some 'authority' alleged to exist outside the processes of experience. Democracy is the faith that the process of experience is more important than any special result attained, so that special results achieved are of ultimate value only as they are used to enrich and order the ongoing process." Thus, democracy "is the sole way of living which believes wholeheartedly in the process of experience as end and as means."[17] Radical means for radical social ends — that's what Dewey called for, with democratic values at the core to steer the process.[18]

Yet individuality is also a well-guarded American value. So to Dewey, while democracy is "a *personal* way of individual life . . . determining desire and purpose in all the relations of life,"[19] our social arrangements "are not means for obtaining something for individuals, not even happiness. They are means of *creating* individuals."[20] A democracy, Dewey insisted, likewise values diversity. This is more than tacit tolerance; citizens must respect different ways of being. This is not only just but, as Dewey saw it, valuable for personal growth. In fact, to Dewey, "inherent in the democratic personal way of life" is the need "to cooperate by giving differences a chance to show themselves," and we do this "in the belief that the expression of difference is not only a right of the other persons but is a means of enriching [our] own life-experience."[21]

Thus, a democracy, naturally and necessarily, values equality. "Belief in the common man is a familiar article in the democratic creed. That belief is without basis and significance save as it means faith in the potentialities of human nature as that nature is exhibited in every human being irrespective of race, color, sex, birth and family, of material or cultural wealth." And recalling his earlier "radical" text, the philosopher went on to say: "To denounce Nazism for intolerance, cruelty and stimulation of hatred amounts to fostering insincerity if, in our personal relations to other persons, in our daily walk and conversation, we are moved by racial, color or other class prejudice; indeed, by anything save a generous belief in their possibilities as human beings and hence in the need for providing conditions which will enable these capacities to reach fulfillment."[22]

Individualism and Dividualism

Individualism does not stand alone at the core of American freedom. So this value raised serious concern for the philosopher because it could threaten democracy itself. The problem, as Dewey saw it, lay in the prevailing "conception of individuality as something ready-made, already possessed, and needing only the removal of certain legal restrictions to come into full play." So Dewey found it important to assert that individuality is a quality we achieve rather than inherit; it is "a moving thing, something that is attained only by continuous growth."[23] And he went to great pains to trace how the philosophical intent of the pursuit of life, liberty, and happiness had been co-opted into becoming an individualistic economic doctrine.[24]

As he tells it, Jeffersonian ideals had migrated away from their agrarian roots and been put through the ringer of the Industrial Revolution, so that politically we ended up with two camps of liberalism: one seeking to protect the individual from the state; the other looking to the state to set conditions under which individuals could realize their potential and possess actual, not just legal, liberty. We see the former in the rugged, I-did-it-myself sort of American individualism. Feeding American competition, it held that "beneficial social change can come about in but one way, the way of private economic enterprise, socially undirected, based upon and resulting in the sanctity of private property—that is to say, freedom from social control." Accordingly, "social arrangements and institutions were thought of as things that operate from without, not entering in any significant way into the internal make-up and growth of individuals . . . treated not as positive forces but as external limitations."[25]

In the latter form of liberalism, social institutions are the means by which we create our individuality, while living in harmony with others, and, siding with this reading Dewey wrote, "The human problem is that of securing the development of each constituent so that it serves to release and mature the other." We grow as individuals when we find healthy ways to live together. He pointed out we had allowed cultural conditions to develop, especially through the workings of the economy, to the point where social cooperation became subordinate to individual liberty, thus this is a problem of American culture.[26] So while "individuals find themselves cramped and depressed by absorption of their potentialities in some mode of association which has been institutionalized and has become dominant," and "they may think they are clamoring for a purely personal liberty," what serves us all is "to bring into being a greater liberty to share in other associations, so that more of their individual potentialities will be released and their personal experience enriched."[27]

Taking up this subject in the 1930s, Dewey blamed the economic crisis on laissez-faire capitalism, which played into the American image of rugged individualism. Provoking a reconsideration of whose potential is nurtured in our society, whose achievements are prized, and whose transgressions are excused, he proposed that if those in power sought to strip people on relief of their voting rights, that should be coupled with the same action against employers who failed to pay their debts.[28] Fast-forward and we end up with Donald Trump, whose claims of individually realized economic power leave us with a society of only winners and losers, with government absolved from responsibility and above the law. To Dewey such staunch individualistic posturing showed little concern for economic equality and liberty among the greatest numbers, which he believed could only be achieved through social control of economic forces.

If we were to live more cooperatively, a common intelligence would be shaped, passed on, and owned collectively. This "intelligence," Dewey knew, "is a social asset and is clothed with a function as public as its origin, in the concrete, in social cooperation."[29] It is present in the mechanic as he carries out his calling and of whom Dewey wrote: "He has lived in the environment in which the cumulative intelligence of a multitude of cooperating individuals is embodied, and by the use of his native capacities he makes some phase of this intelligence his own."[30] We hear Dewey's understanding of social intelligence in the 2012 election campaign rhetoric of President Barack Obama, which so bristled against the rugged-individual ideal, when he said: "There was a great teacher somewhere in your life. Somebody helped to create this unbelievable American system that we have that allowed you to thrive. Somebody invested in roads and bridges. If you've got a business, you didn't build that. Somebody else made that happen."[31] We all profit by being part of a culture of individuals when built on democratic values of social cooperation. Investing in this wider social enterprise pays off, Dewey thought, and from it we all draw benefits.

"The things in civilization we most prize are not of ourselves. They exist by grace of the doings and sufferings of the continuous human community in which we are a link," the philosopher wrote.[32] But the social intelligence on which this depends runs a slow second because of "our ingrained habit of regarding intelligence as an individual possession and its exercise as an individual right."[33] Still, Dewey put his faith in an intelligence held in common. It was as essential to personal liberty as it was to the freedom of the society at large, for "only by participating in the common intelligence and sharing in the common purpose as it works for the common good can individual human beings realize their true individualities and become truly free."[34] Believing we succeed when we all succeed and that the common good is a shared asset, Dewey thus wrote: "The clear consciousness of a communal life, in all its implications, constitutes the idea of democracy."[35]

Common intelligence stood at the very foundation of this country and was right there in the very writing of the Declaration of Independence. So as Dewey traced how Thomas Jefferson's concepts within this document were not his own alone, it was not to demonstrate a failing. Rather, he showed what was "new and significant was that these ideas were now set forth as an expression of the 'American mind' that the American citizen will be prepared to *act* upon," seeing this "*action* as a practical 'experiment'" in self-government.[36] Looking to the same period in history, cultural critic and poet Lewis Hyde cites Benjamin Franklin, who saw "his own inventions in the language of gift exchange, noting that 'as we enjoy great Advantages from the Inventions of Others, we should be glad of an Opportunity to serve others by any Invention of ours, and this we should do freely and generously.'"[37] And writing of the cultural commons, Hyde looks to the common intelligence to be inherited and preserved for all, and which is pivotal in not only the discourse of democracy but also of a creative community.[38]

Making is both individual and collective. "Creativity always has this double nature to it," Hyde writes. "There's always some uniqueness, an individual aspect involved, and there's also some collaborative commonality."[39] We do not act alone as we build onto our past inheritance. Yet in the art world, there is so much pressure on ascribing authorship and defining the parameters of artworks. In the early nineties, as this anxiety was building, artist and writer Steve Durland tried to get a handle on why collaborative, community-based work—which drew upon multiple intelligences and broke down hierarchies among makers and audiences—was causing such a fuss among critics who were thrashing about, trying to locate the artwork, name an art movement, and identify what was new (the ultimate gauge for contemporary art). "If we want to talk about this as a new avant-garde art movement," he wrote, "then it's possible to say it's the first such movement that doesn't challenge the art that has gone before it but rather champions art's intensified application in society." It widens the frame of art rather than erasing other ways of making. And unlike previous art revolutions, the radicalism of this communal art practice lay not in challenging the conventions of art but rather art's infrastructure, as the artist and the community are each a "self-interested participant."[40]

This coexistence of a dual nature of being is present in Dewey as the notion that the "self, or individuality, is essentially social, being constituted not by isolated capacity, but by capacity in response to the needs of an environment—an environment which, when taken in its fullness, is a community of persons."[41] As he saw it, the development of oneself as an individual and as a social being are two sides of the same coin: independent and interdependent. Thus, Dewey's idea of a democracy is also dualistic in that the rights of the individual are in balance with those of the society at large within a constantly negotiated, creative process that is always in flux and continually coevolving. But Dewey's sense of the social self was decidedly nonmodern and non-Western. And he acknowledged as much when he wrote: "The idea that human nature is inherently and exclusively individual is itself a product of a cultural individualistic movement. The idea that the mind and consciousness are intrinsically individual did not even occur to any one for much the greater part of human history."[42]

To understand this dual nature of being, Lewis Hyde has introduced the concept of "dividual": the self as divided or shared with others, as opposed to the individual that is indivisible. He offers the example of Micronesia where "persons are not thought of as having the complexity of the social world outside of themselves, but rather inside themselves. . . . Your identity is dependent upon this surround of other things, which are at least as interior as not."[43] Likewise the tenet of interdependence in Buddhism reminds us of our inherent connectedness by representing it with the weblike model of Indra's net.[44] As Hyde suggests: "If you think about . . . what the Buddhist might say, it's the self that has forgotten the self and, thus, is actually in a different way at home in nature and among other sentient beings."[45]

When we join our sense of self to that of someone else, we realize what Buddhists call interconnectedness, what Hyde calls dividualism, and what Dewey called unity of being. Art gives us a way into this state of consciousness and acting in the world.

Practical Experiments in Making Change

In 1939, Dewey recognized that the actions of totalitarian countries should give us pause to remember that the arts are "an important part of the social conditions that bear upon democratic institutions and personal freedom."[46] He saw how their propaganda agencies used regulations to limit artistic freedom while using images and symbols to define and control culture. That art can be used for nondemocratic purposes was on the mind of Magdalena Abakanowicz, an artist who grew up in Poland during World War II, when she said:

> I wanted to tell you that art is the harmless activity of mankind, but we recall that art was often used for propaganda purposes by totalitarian

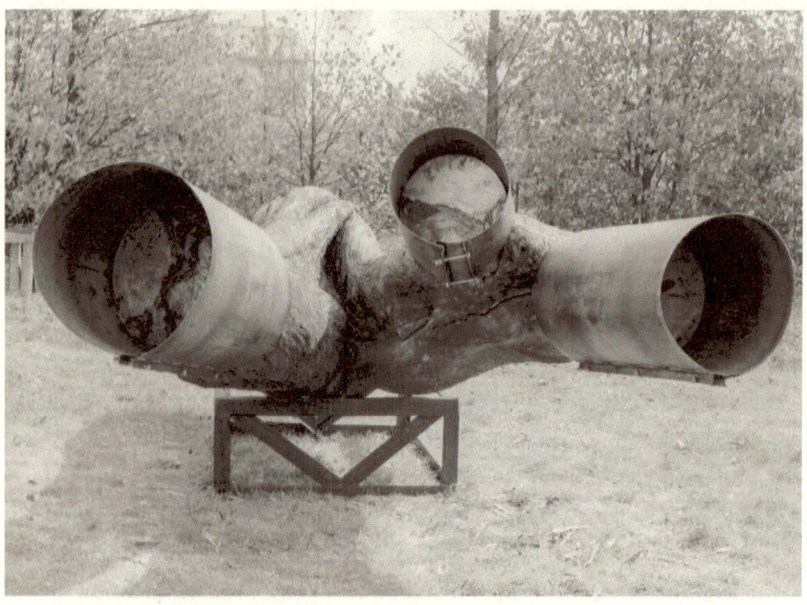

Magdalena Abakanowicz. *Anasta* from the series "War Games," 1989. Wood and steel. Photo: Artur Starewicz, courtesy Marlborough Gallery, New York.

systems. And we remember that Hitler was a painter and used to write poems.

Art will remain the most astonishing activity of mankind deriving from constant struggle between wisdom and madness, between dream and reality in our mind.

Every scientific discovery opens doors behind which are other doors, closed. Art does not solve problems but makes us aware of their existence. It opens our eyes to see and our brain to imagine.

To have imagination and to be aware of it means to benefit from possessing an inner richness and a spontaneous and endless flood of images. It means to see the world in its entirety, since the point of the images is to show all that which escapes conceptualization.[47]

Dewey believed in the importance of art in making a free culture. "The first stirrings of dissatisfaction, and the first intimations of a better future, are always found in works of art," he wrote.[48] To him, art could be a way to imagine and make change. Today socially minded and socially engaged artists offer practical experiments in achieving democracy in our time. Through their practice, exposing injustices and repositioning what is possible is more than just a provocative assertion. It can affect our political and social imaginary.

To imagine differently requires images. Alfredo Jaar has traveled the world seeing things others do not want to see. In 1991, at the Pillar Point Refugee Centre in Hong Kong, it was through the face of one young Vietnamese girl who had followed him. He showed us Nguyen Thi Thuy one hundred times in his artist's book that bears her name.[49] Do we see her now? A few years later he "was in Ntarama, forty kilometers south of Kigali, Rwanda, on August 29, 1994, in the aftermath of a genocide, the third of our century, that claimed one million lives — one million lives — in the face of the criminal, barbaric indifference of the so-called world community." Jaar continued: "How can I forget the vision of five hundred corpses on the ground, rotting under the African sun? How do I change that order of reality?"[50] Traveling to Rwanda twice during that wartime period, between 1994 and 1998 Jaar employed different formats through scores of works in an impassioned effort to bring forward the images he held in his mind. In his thirteenth project on this subject, he struck on *The Eyes of Gutete Emerita*. Then we saw her.

Jaar's works challenge the domain of the documentary photographer but also share in those photographers' frustration with the inadequacy of their medium as it meets viewers' ambivalence. With *Real Pictures* Jaar entombed Rwandan images in archival boxes, providing a description on the lid; he installed them in dark galleries so they became like tombstones and the gallery a cemetery; then he asked visitors to go to an adjacent room to reexamine the press images we had hastily removed from sight. Another work, *Lament of the Images*, was an ode to the loss of sight. Three stories were each represented by white text on black film in a light box: Nelson Mandela's loss of vision as a political prisoner; the buried, inaccessible archive of historic photographs amassed by Bill Gates and now only available in digital scans; and the purchase of exclusive rights to satellite images by the US Defense Department before its 2001 airstrikes in Afghanistan. We will not see them.

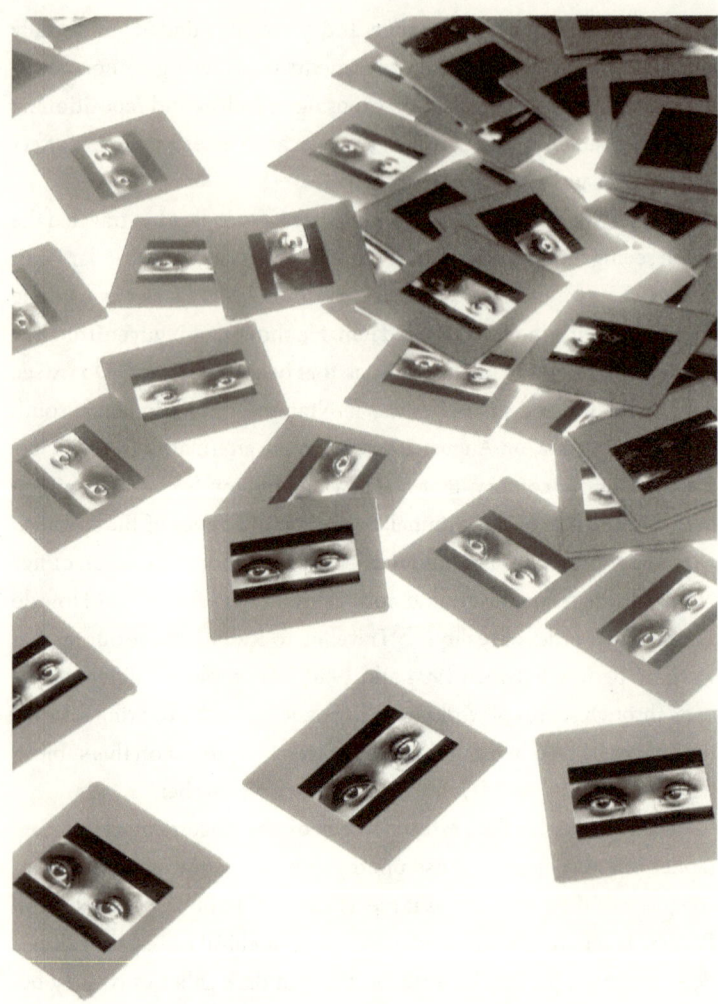

Alfredo Jaar. *The Eyes of Gutete Emerita*, 1996. Illuminated text, light table, and slides. Collection Museum of Fine Arts, Houston, Daros Latinamerica Collection. Photo: courtesy Galerie Lelong & Co., New York, and the artist.

Jaar asks: "What is the future for artists now, the order of reality that they must change now, that is all around us?" "I am not advocating for the art world to correct the dire imbalances of the real world, but I would like to suggest that every effort should be made not to replicate so perfectly those imbalances"; and, driven by democratic principles, he adds, "I am arguing for the inextricability of ethical and aesthetic values."[51]

What would an ethical future look like? Tania Bruguera is one of the most ambitious artists venturing new images of the future. Her practical experiments, like democracy itself, are not theories but ideas in action. Since 2006 she has focused on the plight of immigrants, migrants, and refugees who leave their own culture, by choice or not, and arrive into an uncertain and unstable condition. Her remedies, which she has called "pragmatic utopias,"[52] seek to effect social and political change. That they are thwarted in their implementation need not be taken as a flaw. Their value, according to Dewey, is in imagining solutions.

Bruguera sensationally opened Immigrant Movement Interna-tional, a center for art and activism in a storefront in the Corona neigh-borhood in Queens, New York, in 2010. Yet even a decade earlier, as she herself was thinking of leaving Cuba for the US, she began to work with homelessness, linking this condition to that of immigrants who lose their homeland. Then "coming from Cuba, where everybody's the same, to Chicago, a multinational place, was a shock. This was something that actually marked me a lot. I don't think it was until *documenta* in 2001 that I actually fully understood I had to redefine who I was *as* an immi-grant."[53] When you are an immigrant "you reinvent yourself; you have to learn the language, make new friends, the whole thing." Ten years later, she recounts, "when I went to Paris, I went through the same pro-cess. That's crazy. I thought the immigration experience was one time; you do it once, like virginity. But, no, you go on and on again every time you move."

Being in Chicago was also a politicizing moment for Bruguera. "I realized I had not been political; I was just illustrating politics. I spent many years battling art and activism, and that came out of Chicago because I saw the activist work artists were doing there; it was social change: to be political is not only telling people what happened in a place, but making change." "In Chicago, I really appreciated the culture of working," Bruguera continued. "People have a goal; they're doing it for a reason, not just producing for producing's sake—not in the sense of capitalistic accumulation, like 'what is your improved painting that you're doing right now.' Chicago has a roughness that I have with my work now. It's urgent. That's how I feel. There I literally started defining my practice, attaching a body of thinking to the work by doing research, and understanding that my research was about power and how to deal with power. Before things were just subjects." Then it became "understanding that your art practice is a long-term research, and not just production."

When, in 2006, Bruguera first began working on Immigrant Movement International, the concept was to create an actual site of immigrant empowerment, but her aim became greater: to make change on the level of civil society internationally. So Bruguera simultaneously initiated the Migrant People Party to advocate for basic treatment at the level of human decency for those in precarious situations between nations. In 2014 she called upon Pope Francis to grant Vatican City citizenship for those without a country, a legal status she believes could play a life-sustaining role beyond fleeting acts of charity.

Other artists and architects have tested national identity. Some have formed micronations, landed and not. In 1984, artists in Ljubljana, in then communist Slovenia, banded together into the political art collective Neue Slowenische Kunst (NSK). Its visual arts division, IRWIN, has offered NSK passports over the decades so that others can become citizens of this "state of mind." IRWIN and I had worked together in a counter-Olympics project during the 1996 Atlanta Olympics, staging conversations between the Russian artists, who traveled with them as they made their way across the country by RV, and the American artists they met, all the while signing up NSK citizens. Parodying the totalitarian state in which they once lived, they famously continue to play the game that nations do in a part of the world where borders remain shifting. This proved to be useful art. Some people have crossed borders with their NSK passports, tells IRWIN member Miran Mohar.

Bruguera promotes the concept of useful art, which she dubs *Arte*

Útil, proposing "some solutions for deficits in reality"[54] and stressing that art can transform society. For Bruguera, artists "have the power to transform affect into effectiveness," so they should use it.[55] Like Dewey, who deemed art "the most compelling of the means of communication by which emotions are stirred and opinions formed,"[56] she believes art is an effective means. So in 2015 Bruguera established the Instituto de Artivismo Hannah Arendt with the intent of enabling citizen participation in the changes underway in her native Cuba.

Projects like Bruguera's are also symbols—symbols of the need for change. Dewey did not make light of symbols; he saw them as the best means by which we share the meanings that experience accrues. "Wants and impulses are then attached to common meanings. They are thereby transformed into desires and purposes, which, since they implicate a common or mutually understood meaning, present new ties, converting a conjoint activity into a community of interest and endeavor." Symbols can generate "a general will and social consciousness."[57] And if we are not limited in our definition of art but rather understand, as Durland does, that actions among a community of persons can be an art that "champions art's intensified application in society," then Bruguera's work might be very useful art, indeed.

Yet this all takes time. Dewey recognized that change "does not occur all at once nor completely."[58] Bruguera has come to know this, too: "You have to be very patient." It's a life-long practice. To keep the course, you need to be clearly grounded in values you believe in— Dewey would advise democratic ones—aiming toward "the things you want to change for yourself or your community, the things you care the most about," as Bruguera puts it. Perhaps it is through symbolic acts, actualized as practical experiments, that we can advance toward democratic change in time.

The Politics of Art Appreciation

Art is a way we practice democracy. Democracy can be practiced as an art. Thus, art and democracy were a lot alike to Dewey. Both are embodied, lived practices. Both are creative processes. Both have an aesthetic dimension and, therefore, in our experience of them lies the potential for our transformation. The philosopher also believed that art has the ability to help us develop into better citizens, because art catalyzes change, helping us as well as society to grow and remain vital. Thus, the appreciation of art has a moral and political dimension.[59]

In Dewey's politics of appreciation,[60] a chief attribute of art is its exceptional capacity to evoke empathy. An art student of mine, Zachary Kamin, once wrote: "I've learned that the most important aspect of an art work is observation—particularly selective observation. Observation is a tool used to empathize. When painters paint using observation, they are empathizing. Engaging in empathy is a psychological act made into a physical act when creating art. The painter is not gifting the viewer with a painting but with empathy. Empathy is the action that causes an esthetic experience. An esthetic experience is one which creates an enormous amount of empathy."[61]

Art aids us in understanding others, allowing us to walk in their shoes, embodying them for a time. Additionally, getting out of ourselves can invigorate and reawaken our consciousness. In the case of Kamin, art also helps us understand ourselves in the world as the imaginings of the artist whose work we encounter spurs us on to imagine differently. Bruguera places her body empathetically among others, conscious of her own foreignness, using art to ask us to perceive anew those foreigners we pass everyday and help change how they are seen in the eyes of the law. Seeing our relation to other people and cultures enables us to place ourselves within a larger scheme of things and, thus, to become more conscious of the consequences of our actions on people and the planet. So for Dewey art can fuel progress, showing us the world as it is and inspiring us to imagine otherwise. Art gives us that potential.

When Daniel J. Martinez reflected on his 1993 work with individuals in Chicago's African-American and Latino communities, he was struck by people's willingness "to give themselves over to an idea that had the possibility of . . . failure. Why would you put yourself at risk in such a way?" He posited an answer: "Perhaps this is where the raw power of hope and desire is laid bare. It is the potential to be open to new experiences that can be made possible by these types of exchanges."[62] In such moments, sites of critique become sites of possibility.[63] There is hope on the part of both the participant and the artist, as they share in the making of art and in having *an* experience together, creating and living democracy. Martinez realized such moments are exceptions compared with the shows an artist mounts during a career. "Those deep moments when you can feel something is changing all around you and with the people you are working with, you know you are working on something bigger than oneself as an individual. Those are much rarer and more difficult to find in this world. But that is all that this life seems worth living for. The chance of those moments to come."[64] And, clear on this aim, he adds, "I still think anything is possible and art has infinite potential."[65]

For Dewey, potential was always a beacon. It was at the core of his concept for a public education system addressing the individual student's needs. It was his hope for society, as he kept faith in democracy. He saw hope in imagination and the insight into the human condition that comes with deep and meaningful experience of life and art, experience that ignites the hope we can actually make positive change. Then, in the art of democracy, when the changed consciousness of individuals rises to the level of collective consciousness, there emerges a powerful social engine.

So can artists create democracy? "Democracy begins in conversation," said Dewey, and the "only way to make headway in the international community is to start with the non-political aspects of society — conversation, food, technical meetings, congresses and so on — and end up with politics."[66] Artists do just that as they willingly convene discussions around difficult, vexing problems in thoughtfully conceived ways or bring people together to work on shared endeavors. In these ways they employ Dewey's democratic means — participation, communication, and education — and use them toward democratic ends, and experiences they thereby generate have the power, as Dewey saw it, to be transformed into action.[67]

It is commonplace, Dewey would agree, that food brings people together. Today examples abound where the food and art promote change. Take Michael Rakowitz's *Enemy Kitchen*, first undertaken for a group of New York City high schools, with the artist as chef; subsequent iterations brought together two sides of the US-Iraq war as refugees and former US soldiers in Chicago prepared and served traditional dishes, each participating in "the enemy's culture." *Conflict Kitchen* began as a student project by the Carnegie Mellon University team of Jon Rubin and Dawn Weleski; now this take-out restaurant in Pittsburgh prepares and sells food daily from one of the many countries with which the US is in conflict, communicating to their customers through informative wrappers, the music of the featured country, and by just creating a situation where people can talk to each other. Jasmeen Patheja, an artist-activist, developed *Talk to Me* with her grandmother and college girlfriends to address sexual violence. First coming together to strengthen their own sense of agency, these young women went out on a Bangalore street infamous for rape, inviting men to sit at a table and have a conversation over tea and samosas. At first it was simply though profoundly to engage empathetically, to see each other for the first time as they enacted their humanity. It was not their ambition to devise social solutions but it became that. Describing his project, artist Seamus McGuinness has shared with me that in visiting over one hundred homes throughout Ireland where families had experienced a suicide, he and his collaborator, psychiatrist Kevin Malone, often experienced not a word spoken for hours while many cups of tea were poured. Yet even in silence there was communication. What McGuinness and Malone are achieving in practice and policy has compelled them to make their *Lived Lives* project their life's work.

In these few examples, artists and participants embody the empathy Dewey prescribed. They start with food and end up with politics. And time and again Dewey was very clear that change starts with face-to-face communication. Such simple acts of communication are a human right, a form of freedom to be guarded in a democracy.[68]

Education is another component essential to democracy. So, not surprisingly, artists seeking to bring about change in recent years have employed pedagogical modes in expanded ways, in part looking to the free university lecture-performances of Joseph Beuys. Dewey had promoted education foremost from the beginning of his career. While he knew that education was an important mechanism for instilling democratic values, he knew, too, this does not happen by rote allegiance. We learn to practice democracy at school through discourse and debate, and through our actions. Education needs to be lived. And he knew that its value is not just in learning what democracy is but in learning how to respond to new challenges and confront nagging oppositions, because Dewey knew ignorance is democracy's downfall.

Dewey made his commitment to education first known publicly in an 1897 declaration which, in the spirit of those documents at the foundation of the democratic nation, begins each of its sixty-one paragraphs with "I believe." In it he put forth the values of individuality, giving children tools to think for themselves and to question. It embraced diversity, envisioning a community of peoples that would be formed at school, modeling equality for all individuals. The advance of each child, regardless of class and background was, to him, *the* American dream to be achieved: "I believe that education is the fundamental method of social progress and reform."[69] Then education would thus be not an ideological stance but society's moral duty.

Dewey also inspired education as a great collective experiment in arts education at Black Mountain College beginning in 1933. Visiting in 1940 he observed: "The work and the life of the College (and it is impossible in its case to separate the two) is a living example of democracy in action. No matter how the present crisis comes out the need for the kind of work the College does is imperative in the long run interests of democracy. The College exists at the very 'grass roots' of a democratic way of life."[70] Dewey had hoped this for public schools all across America. Rightly the father of American public education, he had suffered throughout his lifetime the foibles and failings of education in its institutionalized form in addressing the "problem of the relations between individual freedom and collective well-being." "The problem of achieving both of these values without the sacrifice of either one is likely to be the dominant problem of civilization for many years to come. The schools have their part to play in working out the solution, and their own chief task is to create a form of community life and organization in which both of these values are conserved."[71]

To Dewey, education was an art: "I believe that the art of thus giving shape to human powers and adapting them to social service, is the supreme art; one calling into its service the best of artists; that no insight, sympathy, tact, executive power, is too great for such service."[72] Understanding that we are always in a state of becoming as we respond to an ever-changing world, Dewey saw education as a lifelong practice, not just something for the young, and extending far beyond institutional settings. Accordingly today artists contribute greatly to the culture by teaching in formal settings, but also increasingly by setting up their own independent teaching environments with more open and democratic frameworks. The opportunities they create offer participation in creative inquiry, access to interdisciplinary expertise, and robust exchange. In their missions, organization, subject matter, and mechanisms of delivery, these artist-driven enterprises seek to use democratic means to bring about an even more democratic form of education.

J. Morgan Puett runs a summer school at Mildred's Lane in rural Pennsylvania where students, teachers, and artists (with degrees or self-designated as they practice their art) live communally, undertaking every aspect of their everyday lives as a conscious experience — what Puett calls "workstyles" — as they pursue their passions using that piece of land and its local resources in making art. As her cofounder Mark Dion looks at it, shared experience is a way of knowing and learning to generate both knowledge and sociality. "Fostering long-term supportive relationships between students is the most important thing an art educator can do," Dion said.[73] The inability to carry this out fully in the well-regulated environments of accredited schools today (which even free-spirited Black Mountain College might have found challenging) is part of the motivation behind Mildred's Lane.

Brett Bloom of Temporary Services has run summer camps as intensive realignments during which participants can together rethink the assumptions behind the prevailing modes of production and dissemination and learn how to retool the self and society. Meanwhile Thomas Hirschhorn has created libraries and teach-ins around Spinoza, Deleuze, Bataille, and Gramsci. Early in her career, Bruguera's Cátedra Arte de Conducta (Behavior Art School) offered performance art train-

ing in Havana when, having experienced the School of the Art Institute of Chicago, she wanted to find a way to translate performance art
to Cuba and share it with artists there. Even other artists known as the
protagonists of their art believe in and practice a collective process of
discovery. So Ann Hamilton shares her studio with assistants whom she
embraces as comakers and coexplorers, and Katie Paterson's one-to-one
collaborations with experts are colearning experiences.

In the field schools which Ernesto Pujol forms with each new project he undertakes, he transfers skills as he trains performers — Mormon
women in Salt Lake City, Utah; native and nonnative descendants in
Hawaii; citizens in Osnabrück, Germany, and so forth — each time
"recreat[ing] the history of the body in place." In the process Pujol
puts his trust in all "who wish to perform, trained and untrained. I trust
them implicitly, as if I had known them for a lifetime. Our relationship
starts with an act of mutual trust." His school is also a workshop in "our
human right to solitude, silence, and slowness." Like Dewey he knows
that meaning is made in slow reflection, as we return to it after a time, so
he writes: "I want the performers to experience, to give time to experience, to allow experience to take hold. So I prefer for the performers to
withhold talking about the experience until afterwards, after they have
slept on it . . . after it has become a memory."[74]

Importantly, Pujol contemplates what happened to Dewey's model
of education, saying:

> I live in America, where democracy has been dismantled by the cult
> of profit. The middle class has been sacrificed to profit. In order to do
> this, the people had to be un-educated. There was a dismantling of the
> education system as of the 1980s so as to create an increasingly igno-
> rant mass. We currently experience a culture of ignorance, and thus,
> a culture of prejudice. It is hard to work in that environment. The
> heads of the art world fare no better, either in their increasing capitu-
> lation to ruthless commerce, or in their self-complacent bubble of lib-
> eral moralism. The art world has dismissed this mass; the art world is
> afraid of this mass.[75]

So in his own way, Pujol invites citizens into a work he describes as social choreography by which they "create a temporary new reality for [themselves] and for [their] audience, a new reality that may question and challenge [our] ongoing known reality."[76] Artists offer such practical experiments to imagine an alternative reality. The transformative experiences they create, in simple lifeways, nonpolitical gestures that start with meals or meetings, classes or conversations, and end up as politics, make meaning that carries us forward. Through their works of participation, communication, and education, we reconnect. Taking a step toward a common good, we undertake the larger, shared human project that is life. For Dewey, democracy was the way and this can "be accomplished only by inventive effort and creative activity."[77]

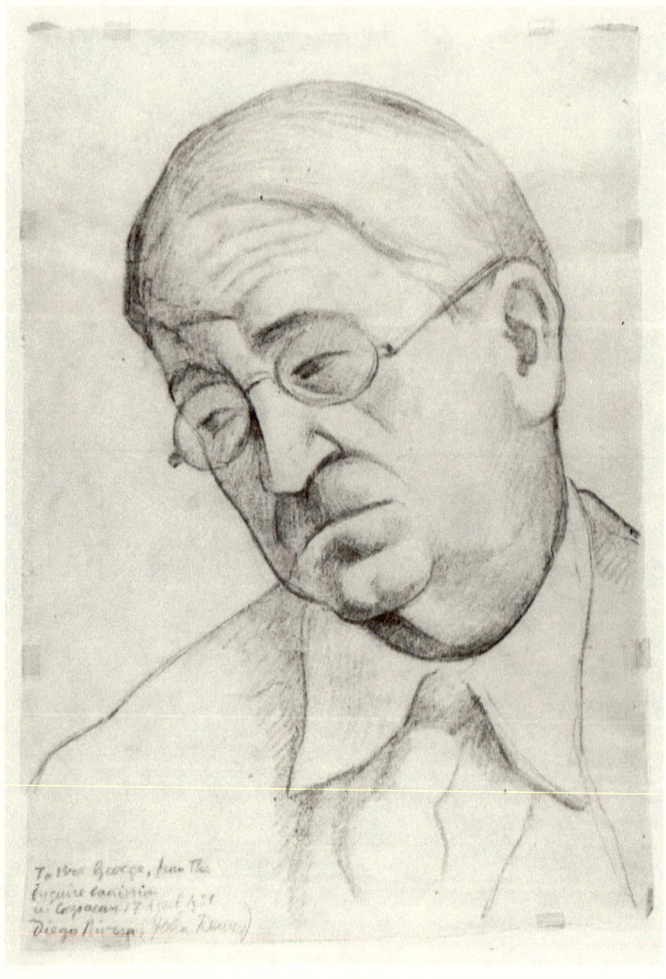

Diego Rivera. *John Dewey*, 1937. Charcoal on paper. Southern Illinois University, University Museum, © 1937 Banco de México Diego Rivera Frida Kahlo Museums Trust, Mexico, D.F./Artists Rights Society (ARS), New York.

5 Participation

John Dewey's lifelong practice as an activist earned him an investigation by the FBI when he was eighty-three. The bureau predicated its task

upon the fact that the New York files reflected that JOHN DEWEY, residing at 320 East 72d Street, New York City, was affiliated with the following organizations: American Committee for Anti-Nazi Literature, sponsor of in 1938; American Society of Cultural Relations with Russia, Vice President of 1933; Committee on Cultural Relations with Latin America, honorary chairman of in 1941; International Relief Association, member of in 1941; League for Industrial Democracy, President of in 1941; League for Industrial Democracy, Vice President of in 1935; New World Re-Settlement Fund, Inc., national sponsor of 1941; American Russian Institute, Board of Directors, 1937; New School for Social Research, member of faculty council, 1941; Council Against Intolerance in America, member of Council in 1941; New York City Conference of a Peoples' Delegation to Biro-Hidjan, sponsor of 1936; Committee for a Boycott Against Japanese Aggression, sponsor of 1941; National Boycott Against Aggressor Nations, sponsor of 1941; American Committee for Democratic and Intellectual Freedom, signed petition to discontinue above organization 1941; Inter-

national Rescue and Relief Committee, national committeeman of
in 1942; Civil Rights Defense Committee, national committeeman
of in 1942; Contributor to COMMON SENSE 1942; National Share
Croppers Week, in March 1942 and February 1943 was a sponsor of;
Workers Defense League, sponsor of 1942; Friends of Democracy
Inc., national committeeman in 1940; International Commission of
Inquiry, chairman of (This commission investigated the Moscow trials
and denounced them as "frame-ups".) . . .

From [name blacked out] the following information was
obtained: Subject was a professor at Columbia University; National
Committeeman, American Civil Liberties Union; National Vice
President of the League for Industrial Democracy; Executive Chairman, League for Independent Political Action; Vice President of the
American Society for Culture with Russia and was on its Delegation
to Russia Committee in 1928. He was a National Committee-man of
the Sacco-Vanzetti League and was on the national committee spon-
soring "Letters of Sacco Vanzetti. He was an endorsor of "Professional
Patriots" and contributed to the NEW REPUBLIC. He was a member
of the National Citizens Committee on Relations with Latin America
and was denounced by MATTHEW WALL of the American Federation
of Labor as a teacher of Communism. He was Vice Chairman of the
International Save Our Schools Committee and in 1918 was a member of the Defense Commission for the International Workers of the
World. He was a member of the Peace, Patriots and People's Lobby
and the National Mooney Billings Committee. He was chairman of
the Mary Ware Dennett's Defense Committee; was the head of a joint
committee on unemployment and was advisor of the Pioneer Youth
of America. He was a signer of the Fellowship of the Reconciliation
Petition for Russian Recognition in 1932. In 1933 he was a Humanist. He is a Communist recommended author and was Vice President
of the Berger National Foundation, a sponsor of the Griffen Building.
He was Vice President of the Fellowship of Faiths. He was chairman
of the action committee of the Conference for Progressive Political Action in 1933. He was a national committeeman of the League
Against Fascism in 1933 and in the same year was a member of the

Free Thinkers Ingersoll Committee. He was President of the People's
Lobby and in 1932 was a lecturer and supporter or the Rand School.
He was an endorser of the Communist, the United States Congress
Against War and in 1933 an endorsor of the Lane pamphlet and editor
of the Progressive Education Association. . . .

[name blacked out] did not believe subject to be a radical but
rather believed him to be very liberal in his views. When questioned
as to what he meant by this, [name blacked out] stated that subject
certainly was not a Communist because he had been chairman of a
commission which investigated the Moscow trials and because he
seemed to be in favor of Trotsky. . . .

At 1 West 89th Street [name blacked out] advised that subject
had been living at that apartment house for the past four years with
his forty year old daughter, JANE, the latter presently being a teacher
in some college. Subject pays $150 per month rental for an eight room
apartment and apparently does nothing but write. . . .[1]

Dewey had been always a writer, completing more than one thousand works in his lifetime. By the end of World War I he had become a
public voice through the progressive political magazine *The New Republic*. He contributed to efforts he believed in, seeking to right injustices
he felt had been allowed to go unchecked. He knew early on that "conditions and events are neither to be fled from nor passively acquiesced
in; they are to be utilized and directed." Favoring a kind of knowing that
"ceases to be contemplative and becomes practical," he saw a problem
with intellectualism that he called "the spectator view of knowledge."
He viewed many of his colleagues as "held back by a lack of courage
from making their knowledge a factor in the determination of the course
of events," instead seeking "a refuge of complacency in the notion that
knowing is something too sublime to be contaminated by contact with
things of change and practice."[2]

In 1992, forty years after Dewey's death, Jacques Rancière said that
participation in contemporary democracy requires one to be a blend of
reformist and revolutionary. He wrote: "The guarantee of permanent
democracy is . . . the continual renewal of the actors and of the forms

of their actions, the ever-open possibility of the fresh emergence of this fleeting subject. The test of democracy must ever be in democracy's own image: versatile, sporadic — and founded on trust."[3] Dewey experienced his first encounter with anarchists, getting into the action during Chicago's 1894 Pullman Strike,[4] and while greatly energized by it and attracted to the cause of the revolutionaries, at heart he was a reformer. Anticipating the path outlined by Rancière decades before those words were ever written, Dewey lived life in democracy's image.

Organizing for Rights

It all began in Chicago, with Jane Addams, in whom Dewey saw courage and commitment to social change. Two months after he arrived in the city in the summer of 1894, he founded the Laboratory School at the University of Chicago, where he also established the Philosophy Department. The next month, he gave a lecture to the Working-People's Social Science Club at Hull-House, founded by Addams and Ellen Starr Gates. Addams and Dewey had met earlier, in Ann Arbor when he was teaching at the University of Michigan; he had first come to Hull-House to lecture in 1892. Now, relocated in Addams's city, he wrote to his wife Alice Chipman Dewey about a talk the reformer gave on the settlement house and her understanding that it was not a "thing but a way of living — hence had the same aims as life itself. . . . Well, Miss Addams hoped this settlement wasn't being started from ambition or the desire to have a settlement, or from the desire to do good. . . . The only way they could take their learning to anyone was by turning it into action so that it could be seen — people were already talked to death & written to death."[5]

"Chicago is as great as the world and we shall live in it together," Dewey said in closing his letter to Alice.[6] Indeed, it was a world constituted by worlds: Austrians, Bohemians, Canadians, Dutch, English, Italians, Irish, Germans, Hungarians, Norwegians, Poles, Russians, and Swedes were among the most numerous in this city of 1.5 million. Dewey observed: "The reception of new elements of population in large number from heterogeneous peoples, often hostile to one another at home, and the welding them into even an outward show of unity is an extraordinary feat." Yet he also regretted that "the consolidation has occurred so rapidly and ruthlessly that much of value has been lost which different peoples might have contributed."[7]

Community organizing and volunteerism arose in force to build new bonds where the long-held continuity of family ties, local customs, and religious connections had been broken in the process of remaking oneself in a new place. Certainly for Dewey, this movement marked something "distinctive . . . on the part of American civilization," "unlike that of old-world charity and benevolence." It was where the individualistic, self-reliant spirit met the communal and social dimension, and where embodied self-agency could be manifest in the will to serve others. If we look "at the activities of a great number of individuals in different spheres (and by individuals I mean voluntary groups as well)," as opposed to the "official side," Dewey said, "there is a scene of immense vitality that is stimulating to the point of inspiration."[8]

Even today, American governance exists side by side with a broad base of volunteer and not-for-profit organizations, bearing the weight of social services to a degree foreign to socialized countries where these are provided, as well as to less free nations where state services are dictated, if they exist at all. For Dewey, however, the coexistence of federal, state, and municipal public functions with independent cultural, religious, and social agencies characterized and contributed to American democracy: "Our faith is ultimately in individuals and their potentialities. In saying this, I do not mean what is sometimes called individualism as opposed to association. I mean rather an individuality that operates in and through voluntary associations. . . . The testimony of history is that in the end such a force, however scattered and inchoate, ultimately prevails over all set institutionalized forms, however firmly established the latter may seem to be."[9]

In setting to work on Hull-House in 1889, Jane Addams framed the project not as one of feeding the poor and attending to their other needs, but of looking to "the most pressing problem of modern life" as she saw it: to bring about "a reconstruction and a reorganization of the knowledge which we possess." She found an ally in Dewey, quoting the philosopher in an article of 1899: "Knowledge is no longer its own justification, the interest in it has at last transferred itself from accumulation and verification to its application to life."[10] Hull-House was founded for the purpose of applying knowledge to life.

"My definition of the settlement," Addams wrote, "is an attempt to express the meaning of life in terms of life itself, in forms of activity."[11] The activities of Hull-House were vast, encompassing four realms, as Addams explained it — the social, educational, humanitarian, and civic.[12] This ranged from healthcare to manual skills training, from lectures and conferences by local and world-renowned figures to concerts and neighborhood dances. Its over fifty clubs, which brought together people with a special interest, knowledge, need, or background, drew American-born, educated men and women, public school teachers and college students into the milieu of the city's poorer immigrant communities. Their interchange led Hull-House to go on to offer college extension courses, house a branch of the Chicago Public Library, and establish an art gallery. Just four years into operation, Addams noted: "Perhaps the chief value of a Settlement to its neighborhood, certainly to the newly arrived foreigner, is its office as an information and interpretation bureau. . . . Without endowment and without capital itself, it constantly acts between the various institutions of the city and the people for whose benefit these institutions were erected."[13]

Thus, Hull-House volunteers were the glue between the population in need and governmental agencies. And while over a thousand people were coming to Hull-House weekly by that time, the larger part of the work was done in the surrounding communities, working in neighborhoods and actually holding accountable the public institutions founded to serve them — for, as Addams politely pointed out, public authorities are "always waiting to be urged to do their duty."[14] When Hull-House residents (as the working associates were called) could not resolve the problem, they took on the government jobs themselves to change the agencies from within.

The issues of Hull-House became Dewey's issues. Everything social was political. Like Addams, Dewey and his wife Alice were staunch supporters of women's suffrage, a long battle not won until 1920. At Hull-House Alice Hamilton and Rachelle Yarro pioneered family planning services and access to abortion, and Dewey became outspoken on the withholding of birth control, calling it yet another incident of "ignorance, prejudice, dogma, routine, tradition, which fights against the spread of new ideas that entail new practices." He appealed to common sense (though even today we seem hard pressed to make that case), saying: "With this particular scientific discovery there arose the possibility of intelligent control of blind natural processes. This is the logic of the birth-control movement. Just as expanding knowledge of electricity brought with it the electric light, telegraph, telephone, dynamo, so scientific knowledge of the transmission of life enables mankind to bring that process under human direction." He fumed that social and political influence was blocking the intelligent use of knowledge that was critical to women's health, continuing: "Meantime, however, individuals are prevented by law and by public sentiment from access to the knowledge which would give them more complete control of their conduct—laws and public sentiment that were formed when adequate scientific knowledge was lacking. How can anyone who believes in education and in enlightenment of the public through education fail to be opposed to this restriction on the flow of intelligence?"[15] The answer was evident to him.[16]

Fighting in 1932 for a Senate bill on birth control, Dewey made clear: "It is aimed at reinforcing all the factors which conserve human life and wellbeing, that of mothers, of children, of families. It is aimed at the prevention of abortion that takes such a toll of human life in this country. It aims at substituting the administrations of competent physicians for the activities of unscrupulous quacks. Can anything more absurd be imagined, than that clinics should be established for the care of women, and that a reputable physician should be guilty of a crime if he gives information as to the location of these clinics, to a woman needing care?" Though pro-life and pro-choice factions continue this very fight today, Dewey had already crafted a resolution: "Organized groups have a right to attempt to dissuade their own members from resorting to contraceptive measures if they are willing to take that responsibility on their conscience. But it is un-American, undemocratic, and despotic, for those groups to attempt to use legislation to create crimes, in order to impose their special moral views upon others."[17] Even when battles were won, they were not put to rest. So Dewey found absurd that no sooner had the "most educated people thought ... biological evolution [was] accepted," than "legislation in Tennessee and the Scopes trial brought about an acute crisis that revealed how far that was from being the case."[18] Today he would find new, and many of the same old battlegrounds, on which to fight.

There were other campaigns, too. Dewey sought tax reform because "the major part of all government revenue is paid by the masses, whose income is not sufficient to enable them to maintain a decent healthful standard of living." In this he pointed out that the system "favored five hundred odd with incomes over $1,000,000" who at the same time benefit by "busily exporting jobs by starting branch factories or moving their plants abroad." The .0004 percent at the top (less than half today's touted one percent) was not paying its fair share.[19] As chair of the National Committee of the Commission of Experts on Money and Banking, Dewey wrote to President Roosevelt urging that the banks be nationalized, citing recommendations adopted a year earlier by the League of Independent Political Action that "would have relieved the banking crisis." Their plan of action, he outlined, would reap one billion in emergency relief funds and five billion for public works. He closed with Main Street vs. Wall Street rhetoric that echoes today: "Such projects could be financed by bonds payable out of higher income and inheritance taxes on wealth in the higher brackets, or if scrip is going to be issued to aid bankers, then let it also be used to aid workers by relief and re-employment."[20] Moreover, seeing the close alignment of the two major political parties with business, he called for a reorganization as a member of the League for Independent Political Action, eventually urging that progressive Democrats start a new party.[21]

Not a cause needing support or civil right threatened went unnoticed. He was a founder of the NAACP in 1909; he helped institute the American Committee for Protection of Foreign Born, the American Committee for the Relief of Russian Children, and the Chinese-American Commission. The FBI seems to have found these of little interest. So, too, slipped by his organizing activities in the field of education, which included, among others, the American Association of University Professors (a union of his own which he founded in 1915, becoming its first president), the New York City Teachers Union, the Committee on Education for International Goodwill, and the Organizing Committee for National Aid to Education. He helped found the American Federation of Negro College Students, convincing Eleanor Roosevelt to chair its Advisory Council.

In organizing for the rights of others, John Dewey and Jane Addams shared a belief that when we do for others, we do for ourselves: everyone's rights are human rights. Hull-House had been established on "the theory that the dependence of classes on each other is reciprocal."[22] Of this greater vision, Addams wrote: "A settlement constantly endeavors to make its neighborhood realize that it belongs to the city as a whole, and can only improve as the city improves."[23] Dewey perceived the meaning this holds, quoting Addams to his wife: "The great awakening of social consciousness in the labor movement was one of the most deeply religious things in modern times — if not the most so. To come in contact with that alone meant an awakening into a new life."[24] Dewey would later develop an understanding of religion not as an organized spiritual tradition but as a quality of human activity. Looking not to miraculous interventions by supernatural forces but relying on faith in human capacities, he would later offer this definition: "Any activity pursued in behalf of an ideal end against obstacles and in spite of threats or personal loss because of conviction of its general and enduring value is religious in quality."[25]

A Contemporary Settlement House

Morten Goll and Tone Olaf Nielsen, a painter and curator duo, founded Trampoline House in 2010 in Copenhagen as a place where refugees, migrant workers, and asylum seekers can rebuild their lives through a range of offered social, educational, humanitarian, and civic services. Like the historic Hull-House, it even has an art gallery. Understanding, as Dewey did, that art gives us access into our and others' worlds, its Center for Art on Migration Politics (CAMP) gives visitors insight into

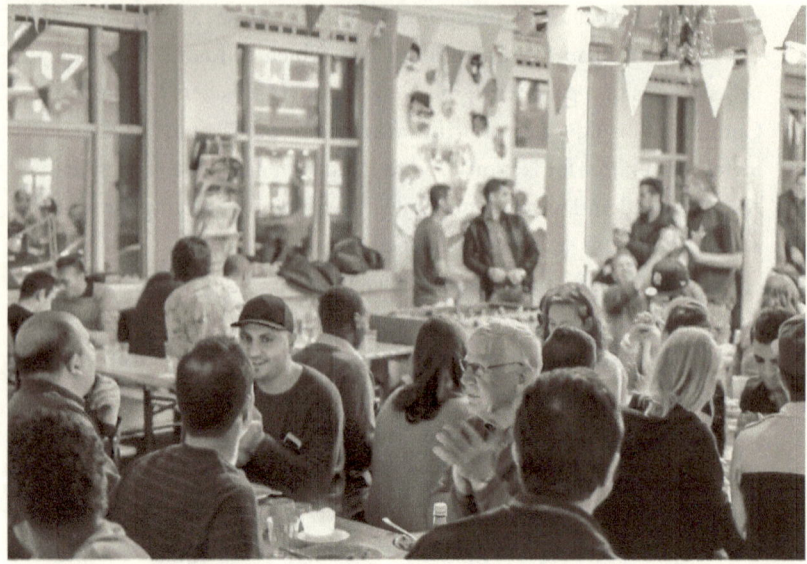

Community dinner in Trampoline House, 2014. Photo: Mikkel Hørlyck, courtesy Trampoline House, Copenhagen.

their own experiences and those of others as they encounter works by artists who themselves endured similar circumstances.

While first a temporary experiment, Goll and Nielsen found they needed to take a long-term view, infusing their work with the energy and belief that come only when one embodies work as an art. Trampoline House could not be "a project," as Goll reflects what this means for social art practice:

> You accumulate experience from each project, but when you move to a new project, there's a loss of part of the knowledge that you experienced and learned. And all of the people who were on the road with you are left without resources, because you took them. Yet the most important resource is the knowledge, the experience. If you do a three-month project in a community, you have the honeymoon and things are really amazing: "Wow, this is possible!" Then you pull out before the problems come. Problems arise when daily life occurs,

and you realize maybe it's not so easy to have this kind of democracy. Trampoline House started as a project critiquing democracy and inequalities in society. Now it's life. And as a living space where different cultures meet, we fail every day, but we also learn something every day.[26]

One of the lessons learned was the nature of social contracts. At first gaining cooperation from the Danish refugee camp authorities, Goll secured funding so the refugees and asylum seekers could travel on day passes to Trampoline House. "We thought we could liberate people from the camps by handing them tickets for transportation reimbursement." But he found that the more people came, the more his generosity appeared to be a show of power. "What was wrong was not giving tickets, but not asking for anything in return. There's no dignity in just being on the receiving end. I was victimizing them once again. This taught me that charity is actually not useful if we want democracy."[27] What was demanded was a human exchange, a commitment to the relationship built on mutual respect among all members of the house. So they set up a system by which users of Trampoline House could participate in making their own future, paying back what they received with, say, three hours of kitchen work, a couple of hours attending Danish class, or teaching something useful to others, whatever skill they could bring to the enterprise.

Hull-House did not trade in charity. "Working people live in the same streets with those in need of charity, but they themselves require and want none of it," wrote Addams. "As one of their number has said, they require only that their inspirations be recognized and stimulated and the means of attaining them put at their disposal. Hull House makes a constant effort to secure these means, but to call that effort philanthropy is to use the word unfairly and to underestimate the duties of good citizenship."[28]

Goll and Nielsen, like Addams and Dewey, have chosen reform over revolution, devising pragmatic solutions to the state's structural problem. But what of the creative lives of this artist and this curator now immersed in the life project that is Trampoline House? "All that I have done here comes out of artistic practice," Goll says insightfully, "and in a way, I feel that Trampoline House *is* art. To me it's art in the sense that we are the only ones who can create a space that works like this. We have different ways of creating possibility for agency and self-empowerment and ownership." Then he continues, "I feel that it would be to the detriment of art as such to disqualify Trampoline House from being art, because if these kinds of projects are possible within art, then we have a bigger playing field. I think it should be allowed to be art."[29] Akin to Steve Durland's revelation that collaborative community projects champion "art's intensified application in society,"[30] Trampoline House widens the frame of art.

Yet because Trampoline House is also urgent life, Goll adds, "I don't really have time to defend it [as art] because we're so busy here." Maybe Jane Addams can help to explain; she said: "The chief characteristic of art lies in freeing the individual from a sense of separation and isolation in his emotional experience, and has usually been accomplished through painting, writing and singing; but this does not make it in the least impossible that it is now being tried, self-consciously and most bunglingly we will all admit, in terms of life itself."[31]

Defending Rights

In *Art as Experience*, Dewey wrote that a civilization is judged by its cultural output,[32] and he prized art as valuable evidence of a society's worth. But he also said, "The best way to judge a culture is to see what kind of people are in the *jails!*"[33] He wanted to make sure the wrongfully accused stayed out. So without expertise or training, Dewey plunged into some of the hottest legal controversies of the early twentieth century.

"Prejudice is a curious word," the philosopher wrote. "It is something that goes before judgment. It is even a kind of foolish and unwise judgment. It is something that precedes judgment, that tends to prevent and to distort it." With his deep and long-considered understanding of the psychology of the human being—what leads us to do what we do—he added, "the very reason that prejudice is so obdurate, so hard to deal with, is that it comes from the irrational part of our nature, the sub-human part of instincts and impulses, fears, jealousies, dislikes."[34]

Looking at the American scene of the late 1920s, he was incensed: "Never have the forces of bigotry and intolerance been so well organized and so active. It is enough to refer to the Ku Klux Klan."[35] Just a few years later, as totalitarian leaders grabbed popular support in Europe, he drew lessons for American society: "In the modern world, every country under some circumstances becomes fertile soil for seeds out of which grow fanatical conflict, intolerance, racial oppression. The attitude which prevails in some parts of our country towards Negroes, Catholics and Jews is spiritually akin to the excesses that have made a shambles of democracy in other countries in the world."[36] He saw history being twisted, writing: "Even when words remain the same, they mean something very different when they are uttered by a minority struggling against repressive measures, and when expressed by a group that has attained power and then uses ideas that were once weapons of emancipation as instruments for keeping the power and wealth they have obtained. Ideas that at one time are means of producing social change have not the same meaning when they are used as means of preventing social change."[37]

Intolerance is what Dewey saw at stake in the trial of Nicola Sacco and Bartolomeo Vanzetti, which drew widespread international attention throughout much of the twenties. Italian-born anarchists, they had been found at the scene of an armed robbery and murder in South Braintree, Massachusetts, in April 1920. Tried in June, found guilty in July, and sentenced in August, they were tried again the next year, put on trial in May and convicted in July. This time both were destined for the electric chair. Working-class and liberal intellectuals joined forces; the Sacco-Vanzetti Defense Committee established at the outset continued its efforts with appeals and hearings; and worldwide protests ensued. Six years later, with the accused still in prison and worldwide sympathy unabated, the Massachusetts governor appointed an advisory committee headed by the president of Harvard, Abbott Lowell, which came to be called the Lowell commission. After two weeks, they determined no new trial should be granted. When the execution took place on August

23, 1927, so too did violent protests and worker strikes as far flung as London and Tokyo, South America and South Africa.

Dewey did not just condemn the legal system but also his peers, whom he believed should have used their intelligence and station to achieve fairness. What meaning did American liberalism have if prejudice could sway the outcome? Three months to the day of the execution, his essay "Psychology and Justice" came out in the *New Republic*, strongly criticizing the Lowell report. Troubled by what this meant about liberals and progressives, the philosopher set out to examine "the psychology of the dominant cultivated class of the country" as well as how the report revealed "the state of mind that must be widespread in the educated leaders of the American public"[38] that could blind them to the injustices that come to those of lesser social rank, where a rush for law and order can overtake a quest for the truth. He opens:

> Sacco and Vanzetti are dead. No discussion of their innocence or guilt can restore them to life. That issue is now merged in a larger one, that of our methods of ensuring justice, one which in turn is merged in the comprehensive issue of the tone and temper of American public opinion and sentiment, as they affect judgment and action in any social question wherein racial divisions and class interests are involved. These larger issues did not pass with the execution of these men. Their death did not, indeed, first raise these momentous questions. They have been with us for a long time and in increasing measure since the War. But the condemnation and death of two obscure Italians opened a new chapter in the book of history.[39]

With clarity and logic, Dewey retraced the commission's mandate from which it had deviated, taking up the mistaken path of judging the accused rather than analyzing the circumstances surrounding the trials. While there were many, his was the most searing of attacks.[40] He observed the rancor that comes when nationality gives way to nativism, saying "I doubt whether there is one person in a hundred who does not associate a large measure of exclusiveness with patriotism." As he went on,

... all exclusiveness is latent contempt for everything beyond its range. The rabies that exultantly sent Sacco and Vanzetti to death is proof of how deeply such patriotism may canker. It extends not only to foreign nations as such, but to foreigners in our own country who manifest anything but the most uncritical "loyalty" to our institutions. Thousands upon thousands of the most respectable element in the community believed they were exhibiting patriotism to the nation or to Massachusetts when they urged the death of men who were guilty of the double crime of being aliens and contemners of our forms of government.[41]

Just as Dewey had claimed, this case indeed opened a new chapter in this country. In 1936, as Franklin Delano Roosevelt was placing restrictions on immigration into the US and employing selective deportation of ethnic groups, Dewey wrote to the president condemning such actions, especially sending anti-Nazi persons back to Germany "although it has been admitted that they would face death or imprisonment at the hands of the Nazi regime." He called for a stop to this "alien-baiting and persecution of the foreign-born."[42]

A year later Dewey was asked to chair a commission himself. This time the accused was exiled Marxist revolutionary and Communist Party leader Leon Trotsky. Trotsky had traversed several countries and, accepting the invitation of Diego Rivera and Frida Kahlo, had joined them in Coyoacán, then the outskirts of Mexico City, where he found other supporters and a hospitable government. And it was there, in April 1937, in those artists' home, that the Commission of Inquiry into the Charges Made against Leon Trotsky in the Moscow Trials convened.

The US Committee for the Defense of Leon Trotsky, seeking to secure his political asylum, knew they required a well-respected, unbiased chair. For this they turned to Dewey, then seventy-eight years old. Vouching for him, one committee member wrote to Trotsky:

Dewey is old, it is true. But his mind is still keen, and his personal integrity beyond question. It was he, you will recall, who wrote the most searching analysis of the Sacco-Vanzetti Case. He will judge the evidence: not, perhaps, as a politician can judge it in a case such as this, but as a scientist and a logician. He will not sleep during the hearings; he will listen with care, will study, will ask questions. It would be a great error to underestimate him.... Dewey is of course not a Marxist; and all his personal integrity and intelligence does not prevent him from being politically on the fence. In that sense we cannot, obviously, be "sure" of him. But with respect to the Trials we can be entirely sure of his opinion, if the truth is made explicit and objective in the evidence and the reasoning.[43]

The philosopher led the charge to "bring to light the objective facts upon which judgment in the case of Leon Trotsky must rest," writing "our sole function is to ascertain the truth as far as is humanly possible." While he admitted that there might have been someone more appropriate than he "for the difficult and delicate task to be performed," he nonetheless conceded, saying: "But I have given my life to the work of education which I have conceived to be that of public enlightenment in the interests of society. If I finally accepted the responsible post I now occupy, it was because I realized that to act otherwise would be to be false to my life work."[44] Dewey knew that to carry out one's life's work is at times to put oneself at risk for what one believes. Indeed he did and, true to form, he was indefatigable in the undertaking.

In the end what became known as the Dewey Commission ruled Trotsky not guilty of Joseph Stalin's charges to which he had been convicted in absentia in Moscow in 1936.[45] However, Dewey seized the moment to clarify that he disagreed with Trotsky's position that the ends justify the means.[46] Still the hearing was seen as a turning point in the history of American liberalism at a time when Soviet leadership came under scrutiny.[47] As for Trotsky, after several failed attempts, he was assassinated by the Soviet Secret Service in 1940 at his Coyoacán home.

There had been other times, before and after, when Dewey fought rulings and sought new legislation. In 1916, he joined the American Union Against Militarism to defend those who spoke out against the war; this organization later became the American Civil Liberties Union, in which Dewey remained active in its defense of civil freedoms. That same year, he spoke out against a proposal to "fix" public education, in part to make citizens of new immigrants, by turning it into "the school of universal and compulsory military service." Dewey saw a country increasingly using fear of the other as a weapon to divide: "I will not ask how much ignorance, and how much of the snobbery of those who, having been longer in this country, look with contempt and suspicion upon new comers there may be in this view . . . or whether the melting-pot metaphor is not itself traitorous to the American ideal."[48] Instead Dewey called upon President Theodore Roosevelt to support national aid, with the goals of wiping out illiteracy and providing continuing and vocational education for all immigrants.

Again in 1929, still fighting the fight, Dewey cosigned an open letter to New York's citizens, urging them to halt the Board of Education from allowing a Junior Unit of the Reserve Officers' Training Corps into high school, seeing it as "a direct entrance of the War Department into our public school system," dangerous to the mind of boys fourteen years of age,[49] forging the value of militarism over democratic core values. Military service, he said, was "the remedy of despair—despair of the power of intelligence,"[50] not the solution. And he became a leading spokesperson for the use of diplomacy as he joined the effort to outlaw war, which led to the 1928 Kellogg-Briand Pact in which fifteen nations condemned war and pledged to resolve disputes peaceably. But Dewey was no fool either, realizing we could not talk our way out of every situation, and, as early as 1933, "he was convinced that Hitler and Hitlerism were 'by all odds the greatest threat to world peace today.'"[51]

Artists for a Cause

Acting on behalf of others is intrinsic to our American way of life, with a belief that advocacy works. When artists join the fight, the form it takes may be unorthodox, but it has the power to create *an* experience. I was part of a team that staged a communal dinner at the Jane Addams Hull-

House Museum, an evolution of the *Final Meals* project begun in 2002
by the Chicago collective Lucky Pierre. For over a decade, they had
been faithfully preparing the last meals as requested by those executed
in Texas since 1982 and made available by the state. On each occasion a
Lucky Pierre member would eat the meal respectfully while their contemplative, solitary act would be videotaped. In 2014, in Addams's historic dining room, some eighty college students, activists, artists, and
persons formerly incarcerated convened to silently partake of one of five
such menus. Afterward they spoke about the issues that had brought us
together.

Among the plenitude of social causes in Chicago, police violence is
paramount, and we are reminded of this weekly as the death count rises,
particularly among African-Americans. Chicago Justice Torture Memorials is an organization formed by artists, educators, and other activists
in 2011 "to honor the survivors of torture, their family members, and
the African-American communities affected by the torture."[52] As in the
case of Sacco and Vanzetti, they looked internationally for support and
deeper resonance by sending out a worldwide call for proposals to com-
memorate this local subject. On the gallery wall of the eventual exhibition, *Opening the Black Box: The Charge Is Torture*, was a list of names
that some survivors signed when they came to see the show.

As someone who desires to hope but waivers on just what a show in
a gallery can do, I found this occasion revelatory, thanks in large part to
one visitor, Martin Reeves. He said,

> As Americans, when you're thrown to the wolves, you don't under-
> stand how it can be that you're wrongfully convicted, that you're put
> in prison. And you walk the yard many days trying to figure out how
> [you] got here. This project brings light not to how you got there, but
> to how you try to get home.
>
> To me, the exhibit means recognition. We all know in the world
> that recognition means a lot. If you accomplish something, you want
> to be recognized. And that's what that wall means. When I signed my
> name on that wall, that wall meant freedom.[53]

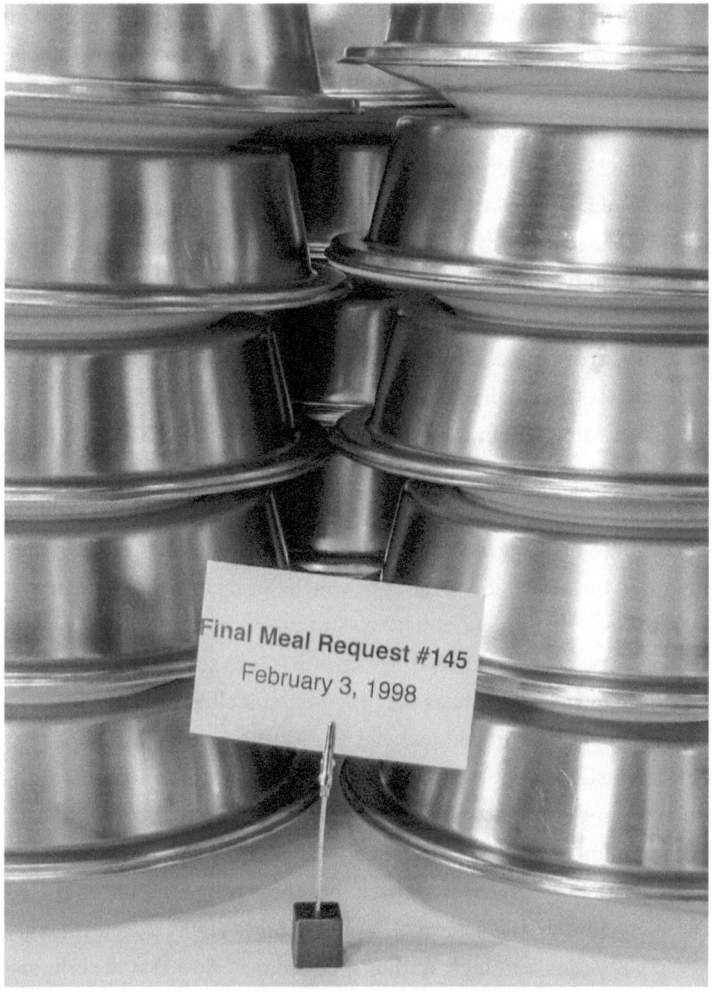

Lucky Pierre, *Final Meals*, 2014. Jane Addams Hull-House Museum Dining Hall.
Photo: Ricardo Phillips, courtesy School of the Art Institute of Chicago.

Maybe art and exhibitions can matter. A year later, the Chicago Justice Torture Memorials' concerted, strategic, and collaborative work led to the City of Chicago's passage of a reparations ordinance, the first in any US city.

There are other artists' projects that take up this cause in Chicago.

Laurie Jo Reynolds was the visible, driving force behind the 2013 closing
of the Tamms Super-maximum Security Prison in southern Illinois.
Dubbing her work "legislative art," she began by using poetry—sending
poems to every prisoner at Tamms, where virtually all human contact
was denied—then detailing their experiences of what it was to be in isolation. Making the case that solitary confinement amounted to torture,
she won the support of elected officials—most prominently, Governor
Patrick Quinn—health professionals, and even the wardens. Her empathetic imagining of what their lives were like in prison, backed up with
evidence, drove the campaign, instilled communication among parties
that had not been in dialogue before, and effected change.

Connecting communities on the inside and outside, artist Sarah
Ross has led Chicago's Prison + Neighborhood Arts Project since 2011,
bringing teaching artists and scholars into Stateville Maximum Security
Prison. This format revives the program of artist-educator Margaret Burroughs in the sixties and seventies[54] which during that time was viewed
by prisoners and the penitentiary system alike as both revolutionary and
reformatory. With artists serving a critical role as teachers, Burroughs's
vision gained momentum as the program built alliances with the city's
Black Arts Movement and fostered relationships with educational and
cultural institutions. Their exhibitions, poetry magazines, theater pro-
ductions, and concerts were not only forms of expression but also means
of communication that transgressed the prison walls. Meanwhile the
revenues they generated went back into these programs and to the incarcerated artists themselves. These exchanges "represented mobility
and possibilities seemingly unthinkable today,"[55] now that the criminal
justice system focuses on keeping people locked up rather than return-
ing them to society.

The personal and social effects of art experiences require time to unfold.[56] Experience is longitudinal, Dewey tells us. And with this in mind
we can appreciate that social practice is not the only art that acts on us
socially; it is but one node on a longer continuum of aesthetic experiences. "Many private acts are social," Dewey wrote; "their consequences
contribute to the welfare of the community or affect its status and pros-

pects." "In short, private acts may be socially valuable both by indirect consequences and by direct intention."[57] This thought was later echoed by John Cage when he wrote: "Art instead of being an object made by one person is a process set in motion by a group of people. Art's socialized. It isn't someone saying something but people doing things, giving everyone (including those involved) the opportunity to have experiences they would not otherwise have had."[58]

Dewey felt that, fundamentally, "human beings have impulses toward affection, compassion and justice, equality and freedom." Likewise shared "are the emotions that arise from living in conditions of inequity, oppression, and insecurity. Combination of the two kinds of emotion has more than once produced those changes that go by the name of revolution."[59] So he reasoned we should only naturally want to act on positive impulses, driven by progressive values, and have an effect on the larger scheme of things, make our contribution. In fact, to Dewey, this is the job of all modes of inquiry — to set in motion processes of discovery and change — but in this, art is exemplary and artists, imbued with open minds,[60] can be effective. Such work "would not only accomplish something toward social health but it would accomplish a greater thing; it would forward the development of social intelligence so that it could act with greater hardihood and on a larger scale."[61] This is how artists participate in the world. To Dewey, this is also how we all can participate in the art of life.

Participation has long life roots. In the early twentieth century, participatory democracy gained strength as Dewey defended what it could bring to pass if we embody and act on its values. Long before participatory democracy was evoked in the communicative theories of Jürgen Habermas, and long before it was a method of bridging ethnic and class disparity through European Union–funded cultural projects of democratic engagement, civic participation, and social innovation, there was Dewey.[62] Dewey was always clear on why participation mattered: "Ours is the responsibility of conserving, transmitting, rectifying and expanding the heritage of values we have received that those who come after us may receive it more solid and secure, more widely accessible and more generously shared than we have received it. Here are all the elements for a religious faith that shall not be confined to sect, class, or race. Such a faith has always been implicitly the common faith of mankind. It remains to make it explicit and militant."[63] Through his participation, Dewey put his faith into action.

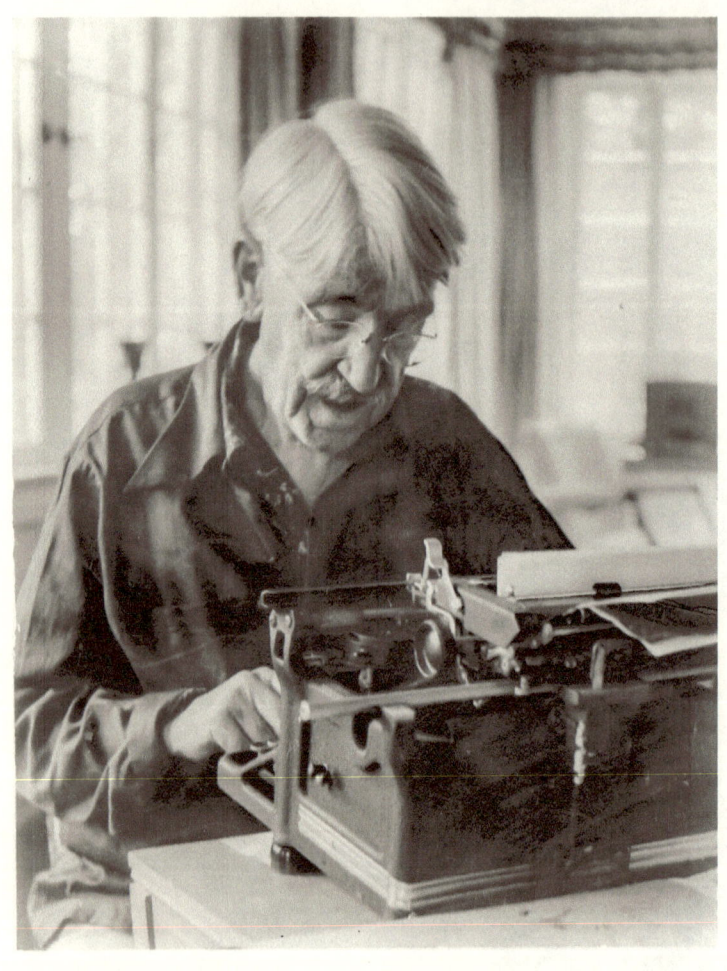

Dewey at the typewriter, n.d. Special Collections Research Center, Morris Library, Southern Illinois University, Carbondale.

6 Communication

Experience is the currency of communication. And experiences held in common are the glue of association, membership, and allegiance, Dewey thought. But he also knew that we are part of something beyond our own and even social experiences, joined by a wider net of being that enables us to imagine what it is like to be somewhere we have not been, what it was like to live during a time other than our own, or to know people we have not met, as we tap into a continuity of human existence. This connection gives rise to the experience of empathy that Dewey believed was foundational to life because of the moral questions and actions it provokes. Empathy moves us to care. At the same time there is much we pass over every day, distanced and distracted, unable to assist, or overexposed to all-too-frequent tragedies.

A blog posting caught my eye: "Empathy Won't Save Us in the Fight against Oppression."[1] The writer oscillated between frustration and contriteness as she reflected on her own unkind actions and disillusionment, concluding that difference cannot be bridged: "Empathy is inherently limited in that it only goes as far as one can imagine, and one's imagination is necessarily bound by [one's] experiences." Really? Not to the philosopher *of* experience for whom activating our imaginations so importantly enables us to exceed our own terms. But in this blogger's assessment, "Empathy is a tool that helps us to become better people, but it is only that. Empathy is not our saving grace."

"Can there be true empathy in art?" mused artist Iñigo Manglano-Ovalle.[2] "To me this is the big issue right now. But if we talk about the intentions of this artist, we can end up divided in terms of black and white, and brown and white. To me, the only way to begin to actually deal with the horror of the war that we're currently living in, is to find a possibility in which empathy and alignment has a place."

Poet Lyn Hejinian has written of engaging with her creative community "around questions of grounds and goals, of dialogue and efficacy, and to some extent [her community] aspired to an increased impersonal freedom for everyone." She added such engagement was "an admittedly utopian enterprise," yet "it was intrinsic to our poetics, and its clear aim was to improve the world."[3] So poetry will save us?

Hejinian explains: "The grandiosity of that ambition may at first glance seem laughable. But it is only so if one assumes that 'to improve the world' requires that one improve it forever." "But the fact of the matter is that the world requires improving (reimproving) every day."[4] And the poet gives insight into the role we can play in the larger human condition, a role Dewey sought to personally demonstrate was not hopeless, when she writes: "To improve the world, one must be situated in it, attentive and active; one must be worldly. Indeed, worldliness is an essential feature of ethics. And, since the term poetics names not just a theory of techniques but also attentiveness to the political and ethical dimensions of language, worldliness is essential to a poetics. . . . Poetics entails involvement in public life."[5]

Art had everything to do with the world for Dewey. As art springs from experiences in the world and then returns to it, it has an effect. While it is true that we would be paralyzed if we felt empathy for everything we are exposed to at every moment, we can transform ourselves by what we choose to actually experience. Art helps us do that. The changes we decide to enact are up to us; it is a matter of will, opportunities, perseverance, and more. But Dewey was clear: we are changed when we share in the larger human community. Just as aesthetic experiences reconnect us with our humanity, empathetic experiences keep us human. Indeed,

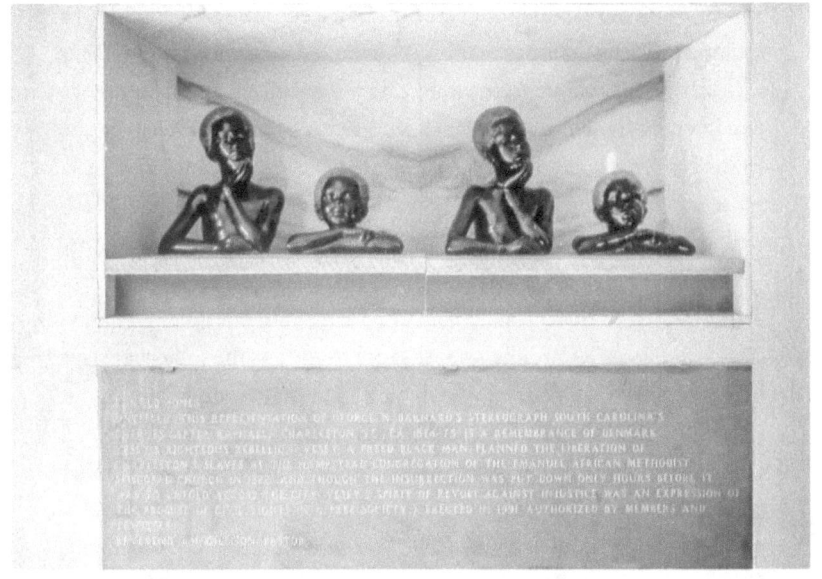

Ronald Jones. *Untitled (This representation of George N. Barnard's stereo-*
graph South Carolina Cherubs [after Raphael], Charleston, S.C., ca. 1874–75, is a
remembrance of Denmark Vesey's righteous rebellion. Vesey, a freed black man,
planned the liberation of Charleston's slaves at the Hampstead congregation of the
Emanuel African Methodist Episcopal Church in 1822. And though the insurrection
was put down only hours before it was to unfold across the city, Vesey's spirit of
revolt against injustice was an expression of the promise of civil rights in a free
society.), 1991. Emanuel African Methodist Episcopal Church, Charleston, South
Carolina. Photo: John McWilliams, courtesy Spoleto Festival USA, Charleston,
South Carolina.

at times they are one and the same. So Dewey put his trust in human nature, trusting that empathic communication was essential, that it could
change the world.

A Shared Experience

For Dewey, shared experience "is the greatest of human goods."[6] Art
provides a way to share experience because it enables us to feel empathy for others. He wrote: "Works of art are means by which we enter,
through imagination and the emotions they evoke, into other forms of
relationship and participation than our own."[7]

That was the experience of art historian Rebecca Lee Reynolds of a sculpture by Ronald Jones that I commissioned for the exhibition *Places with a Past*. She shared: "As a white Charlestonian, it was unlikely that I would ever experience an AME church, but it was art that enabled me to start to cross color lines in Charleston. . . . The experience gave me a sense of opening up to different points of view, to different lives, to listening and learning."[8]

As is my curatorial practice, the artist and I had undertaken the process together. In this instance, Jones had arrived to our first meeting in Charleston, South Carolina, with the idea to address the subject of slave insurrectionist Denmark Vesey, who in 1822 unsuccessfully carried out a rebellion there. With no immediate connection to this subject, I had come with a book on the nineteenth-century American photographer George N. Barnard from an exhibition I had fortuitously seen the day prior. Having chronicled the Civil War and published *Photographic Views of Sherman's Campaign* in 1866, Barnard resettled to Charleston and set up a portrait studio, and it was there, during the first years of Reconstruction, that he was inspired to represent the new hope for an equitable future. Of this series, there is no image more moving than his *South Carolina Cherubs*. Based on a detail from Raphael's *Sistine Madonna*, it depicts two freeborn African-American boys, arms crossed, leaning on a ledge. For Jones, a master of the art of appropriation, this was an image ready-made.

The next move for Jones and myself was to locate the church from which Vesey had carried out his plans; this was the intended siting for the work, but the task proved more difficult than expected. Finally I suggested we use the most prominent Black church, Emanuel African Methodist Episcopal (AME) Church, also known as Mother Emanuel,[9] which happened to be right across from our hotel. Knowing that contemporary art can be seen as subversive (or at the very least problematic), I decided we should check it out unannounced, so we let ourselves in through an unlocked ground-level door. We looked around and eventually found our way up to the main church when suddenly we were welcomed by the presiding pastor, Reverend Gillison. We stated our mission. He proudly announced—"You *are* in Denmark Vesey's church!" Mother Emanuel is where the congregation came to find a permanent home after decades of fleeing hate-motivated destruction.

As we explained the project, the Reverend then asked: "Whatever do you suppose white people would think of a memorial to Denmark Vesey? You expect that they would be comfortable with that?" As Jones recalled, "his undertone wasn't difficult to translate. When he spoke those words, I heard him ask, 'What do you expect white folk would think of honoring a black revolutionary?' It made quite an impression on me, because it was the first time I felt to be on the receiving end of hatred and suspicion." We had been prepared to be on guard if art critics thought we were being merely politically correct; we could have expected challenges from the Black congregation for being a white artist and white curator presumptuous enough to represent Black history; but we had not expected retaliation from the white community.

On June 17, 2015, Dylann Roof also went through an unlocked ground-level door of this church and was also welcomed by the pastor, Reverend and state senator Clementa C. Pinckney, before he killed him and that of eight parishioners. In the subsequent days Reynolds turned to Jones's work:

> I don't know any of the members of the congregation at "Mother Emanuel," or have personal connections to the lives that were lost, but I know this artwork. And this past week I have been thinking a lot about it. It reminds me that in times of crisis, art can offer refuge. The killings were heinous and incomprehensible. If I really think about what happened in Charleston, tears start to well up and my instinct kicks in to stop the tears. Coming back to Jones's artwork is calming and stabilizing. I remember to side with love, not hate. These marble busts offer witness and solace alike. . . .
>
> Jones's sculptures watched Roof and every visitor or congregation member who was welcomed into the sanctuary, and who will continue to be welcomed. They watched the tragic sacrifice of nine more lives. But ultimately, they are watching us. They remind me that site-specific

art can do real work. In this case, the sculptures not only commemo-
rate the struggles of the past, but also bear witness to their continued
relevance and look toward the struggles of the future.[10]

The artist could never have imagined his work's later relevance, but it re-
sounded anew in a wave of empathy. "Because the objects of art are ex-
pressive, they communicate," Dewey wrote. "I do not say that communication to others is the intent of an artist. But it is the consequence of
his work—which indeed lives only in communication when it operates
in the experience of others."[11] This work by Ronald Jones was not meant
to be a memorial to a contemporary event, but now it is.

I didn't see Reverend Gillison again after this project was completed in 1991 until he spoke from the pulpit of Mother Emmanuel during a televised service on the Sunday following the shooting. Later that
week, he was on stage when Barack Obama gave a commanding eulogy
of Reverend Pinckney. The president also said the state of South Carolina is "one of the most neglected areas in America." We are able to ne-
glect what we do not see. Seeing and blindness were major themes of
his speech. But it is empathy that enables us to see what we did not before. President Obama also sang *Amazing Grace*. Maybe empathy *is* our
saving grace.

To the philosopher, we practice empathy to feel our humanness
through our shared vulnerability in open, truly experienced moments.
And Dewey knew great loss, including that of his two young sons:
Morris, age two, died of diphtheria during a family excursion to Europe;
ten years later, eight-year-old Gordon died of typhoid fever on another
European trip. Dewey's vulnerability became his strength. We see it in
his openness to others, sharing his ideas and contributing to their work;
we read it in his committed prose, at times peppered with frustration
and sarcasm.

Empathy causes us to feel and to care. When we receive art in a
caring way—giving ourselves to be present and fully situated, attentive
to the world of which we are a part—then empathetic, aesthetic experiences transpire. We are transformed.

Connectedness

Shared attention is the basis for empathy, as we temporarily enter into another's world. "Once the person-world complex is taken as a unit," psychologist Susan Oyama writes, "it becomes clear that empathetic connection doesn't require a *peeping into*, or even, as the dictionary definition would have it, *feeling into* another person; it is enough to share that person's world, in this particular person-referenced sense," so that it is possible to "end up feeling as the other feels, not just discerning those feelings."[12] Oyama then asks us to contemplate the possibility of a "self-world unity," as she calls it: "what if the surrounding world is not just where we are located, but is part of us, just as we are part of it?"[13]

For Dewey, this was true: we are the environment, and the environment is us. "Unity of human being," he called it. Moreover, for the philosopher, modern science had allowed us to verify this reality as a fact of human existence that enables us to reevaluate and retool our understandings. In 1937 he pressed this understanding at a convening of physicians:

> The boundaries by which we mark off a human being as a unit are
> very different from the energies and organization of energies that
> make him a unified human being. We can observe the boundaries at
> a single moment. We can grasp the unity only, so to speak, longitudi-
> nally — only as something that goes on in a stretch of time.[14]

Sensing how critical this is, he implored the doctors to take heed of their patients' "interaction with what is going on outside the skin," as well as inside, "with that which is called the *environment* — if we are to obtain a genuine conception of the unity of the human being."[15] Thus, to Dewey we not only function as a mind-body unity, but also in relation to each other and the world at large. When we comprehend this and act accordingly, developing our senses of unity within ourselves as well as with the world, we become healthier and contribute to the health of society and the planet.

It is in such moments that we sense our part in the human community, albeit fleetingly. "The self is always directed toward something beyond itself and so its own unification depends upon the idea of the integration of the shifting scenes of the world into that imaginative totality we call the Universe."[16] Katie Paterson seeks to make manifest such connectedness in *All the Dead Stars*, a mapping of the approximately 27,000 recorded extinguished stars. She evokes the grand scheme of the exchange of matter in the cosmos: we are stars, and the stars are us. On earth, she finds this presence at the cemetery in Koyasan, Japan, where she experienced "a vibrancy. The energy is managed, like a garden, and it is still growing. It is a visualization of open heart, love to others, channeling light and energy, compassion rippling out in spheres back in time."[17] This is the gift Paterson gives to her viewers as she offers them a means to inhabit time, to move back and forward into the longitudinal space of which Dewey spoke. This is the consciousness that "takes up into itself meanings covering stretches of existence wrought into consistency."[18] But to achieve this, for Paterson, making art must be an act of compassion.

Compassion and empathy are human reactions that evidence our larger being; enlarging it still, they reaffirm at once the knowledge that we are not alone and that we will not always be here. The connectedness we share within energetic fields stands at the core of our individual and social being. It also shapes our democratic ideals and, thus, our political actions. As Dewey wrote soon after World War II:

> Each generation must rededicate itself to the task of creating a better America than that which we inherited or we shall surely leave it worse. In this period of uneasy peace, we must not neglect the enemy within, if we are to be true to our trust. The misleaders who attempt to create disunity and hatred among Americans are more numerous than most of us realize. Every community has those who preach hatred and discrimination against Americans who happen to be darker skinned, speak with an accent, or share a minority faith.
>
> These misleaders influence millions with their philosophy of hate. They work untiringly to exaggerate racial and religious differences and

to increase tensions founded upon misunderstanding. They would set
Protestant against Catholic, white against Negro, Christian against
Jew, native born against foreign born, capital against labor. . . .[19]

Dewey advised that we "stand against those false Americans who
would recreate our country on totalitarian lines, whether of the right or
left."[20] Without the understanding of others that empathy bestows, we
are doomed.

The Art of Conversation

We have communication tools, but "thoughts . . . are not communicated,
and hence are not common," Dewey mused about modern devices and
their speed.[21] While he appreciated these new instruments, he feared
they lacked human qualities, sensing the ambiguity of technology to
both draw us together and pull us apart as it enables conversations beyond geographical immediacy, yet interrupts experiences in real time.
Now we have even more, *and* they are faster. Moreover, some research
is finding that these new technologies inhibit our neurological ability to
make connections, decreasing our capacity for empathy. As our focus
decreases, we lose our conversational attention, according to clinical
psychologist and sociologist Sherry Turkle. But she says: "When you
speak to people in person, you're forced to recognize their full human
reality, which is where empathy begins."[22] Thus, she concludes: "We are
not talking to each other with full attention."[23]

The art of conversation requires attention in order to fulfill the
human impulse to make meaning. As we increase this ability to go beyond ourselves, we participate in the world, sharing experiences and
"making common what has been isolated and singular."[24] Though
Dewey felt a cult of speed gain ground, he continued to put his faith
in what he called face-to-face communication. This is the most effective means through which to achieve in the "deepest and richest sense
a community."[25] To "learn to be human is to develop through the give-
and-take of communication an effective sense of being an individually
distinctive member of a community; one who understands and appre-

ciates its beliefs, desires and methods, and who contributes to a further conversion of organic powers into human resources and values."[26] To lose that connectedness erodes our humanity.

The art of conversation is a continuous fact of life. "Conversation is fundamental," writes Michael Brenson, echoing Dewey. While understanding that conversation "is part of the machinery of culture, of society, of the self," Brenson makes clear that we need others different than ourselves to enlarge and make us whole.[27] How can we accomplish such a task without empathy and an appreciation of our connectedness? On a personal note, he offers some evidence in his own working method: "I cannot imagine the process of thinking apart from conversation. The way I work out an essay or lecture always involves internalized as well as real conversation with other writers or friends." In turn, for me, Brenson has been someone with whom I have had many conversations, connected through what he calls "a need for common probing. It is driven by a belief in the value of attentiveness."[28]

When in 2010 Marina Abramović sat in the atrium gallery of the Museum of Modern Art for ten weeks, facing visitors one by one throughout the day, what need did she fulfill for those who queued for hours to sit in silence with her? Eight years earlier she lived for twelve days within three raised cubicles in the Sean Kelly Gallery in New York. Its title — *The House with the Ocean View* — connoted the oceanic feeling or consciousness of connectedness to others, an experience that Sigmund Freud thought we outgrew with maturity but Dewey reasoned was an ultimate sign of wisdom. Abramović drew throngs who came to see her bathe, sit, sleep; some stayed for hours; some came every day. She shared with me that those experiences quietly transformed her: "You really understand reality in a different way because it opens up in front of you."[29] And what did visitors take away from these encounters, looking at another human being in all her vulnerability? Did they see their own?

Art can be a conversation we have with ourselves or with others when the work gives us permission to slow down and pay attention, as Ann Hamilton says, and have *an* experience. Just as Dewey perceived, art is a powerful means of social communication. Brenson observes: "Maybe this helps to explain why after sustained concentration in art

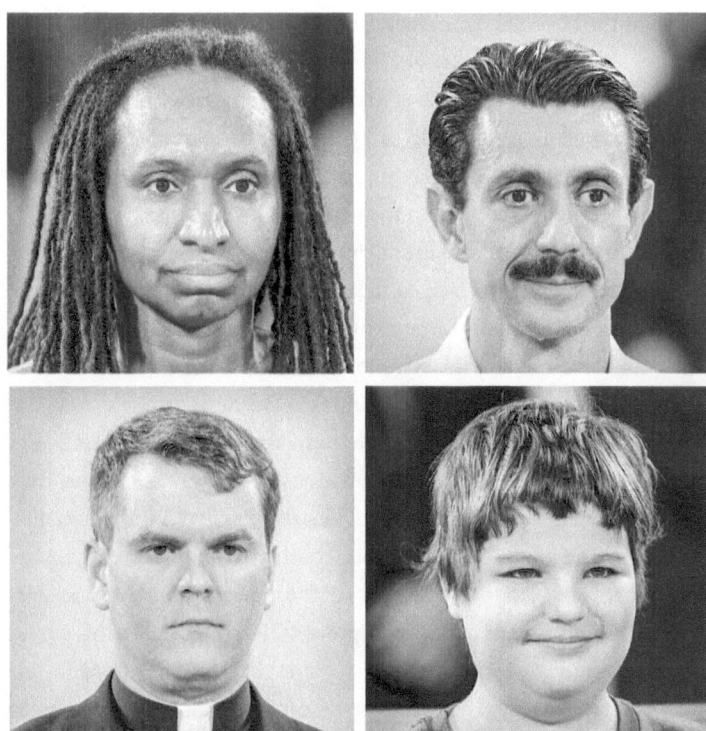

Marina Abramović. *The Artist Is Present*, 2010. Museum of Modern Art, New York, New York. Photos: Marco Anelli, courtesy of the Marina Abramović Archives, New York.

spaces people may suddenly become acutely aware of everyone else around them, who, even as strangers, seem somehow *with* them, and why the encounters with art that seem the most internally intense also therefore seem to have the most social potential. Why the most irreplaceable private experiences with art become at some point insufficient and the most intimate journeys are likely to generate a hunger for collective communication. Why each artist who matters brings into being a potential community."[30]

In his characteristic axiomatic way, Dewey not only saw that art is a vehicle for communication but also that "communication is like art."[31] In each instance, the artist and viewer, or speaker and listener, exchange places as they become empathetically attuned, inhabiting the other for a time. Like the creative process, conversation is unscripted. So to practice communication as an art is to develop the capacity to listen in the process as well as speak.[32] Or, as Dewey saw it, "part of the miracle it achieves is that, in being communicated, the conveyance of meaning gives body and definiteness to the experience of the one who utters as well as to that of those who listen."[33]

Yet Dewey's face-to-face communication is not some cozy conversation but a real working-through of ideas. It is more than the transmission of information; it is the common probing of which Brenson speaks. Bringing consciousness to conversations — assuming Turkle's conversational attention or Hejinian's situatedness, attentiveness, and active engagement — can trigger a transformative aesthetic experience in us. Then and only then does communication, like art, carry with it the potential for imaginative thinking. So no wonder artists attend to the myriad of situational details, the very artfulness of the conversations they create as works of art and as part of social art projects. For the curator, this comes into play, whether attending to the ambience in the gallery or caring for the site in less bounded projects; for me often this also involves staging conversations among constituencies, because conversation-as-art is always a means of having an experience together.[34]

It is through communication we can create community, Dewey thought. Communication is the way to build democracy. As a social idea, as well as political system of government, democracy is "incarnated in human relationships," causing it to be "not an alternative to other principles of associated life. It is the idea of community life itself."[35] Yet Dewey's community depends on empathy.

Dewey's stand on empathy, evident from his earliest writings, may seem far from the fiery evocations of Chantal Mouffe's agonism a century later. Yet for both, democracy is an ethical question urging our enactment. So while Dewey did not want to erase difference into a homogenous America united by sameness, so too he was a realist and knew that strife is necessary to bring about political and social growth. Thus, establishing common ground through conversation would be only a temporary condition in a continually fluctuating world, because conflict is continually present if peoples of disparate cultural values are to each come to play a part. Likewise Mouffe pressed for an understanding of pluralism in democracy, writing: "It is by finally acknowledging the contradictory tendencies set to work by social exchange and the fragility of the democratic order that we will be able to grasp what I have argued is the task confronting democracy: how to transform the potential antagonism existing in human relations into an agonism."[36]

As a contentious writer and pugnacious, participating citizen, Dewey never gave up the fight. His democracy was not theory but an unending practice. He understood that in order to advance the practice of democracy there would always be tension. "To discard the illusion of a possible reconciliation of ethics and politics and to come to terms with the never-ending interrogation of the political by the ethical, this is indeed the only way of acknowledging the democratic paradox," was Mouffe's conclusion.[37] Dewey might well have agreed.

Faith in Intelligence

In a small but mighty opus, *A Common Faith*, published in 1934, the same year that *Art as Experience* appeared, Dewey made his case for putting faith in intelligent cooperative action. This work was in part a treatise on religion. Dewey sought, once and for all, to expunge all hope in supernatural powers, as he distinguished "religion" as an institution from "religious" as a quality of experience. He reasoned that, in a corollary to the way works of art can offer aesthetic experiences, religion could offer religious experiences. However, the religious experience, like the aesthetic experience, is found much more widely: "Many a person, inquirer, artist, philanthropist, citizen, men and women in the humblest walks of life, have achieved, without presumption and without display, such unification of themselves and of their relations to the conditions of existence."[38] And these experiences to Dewey had a genuine sense of the religious.

Some forty years earlier, Jane Addams had spoken of experiences that have a sense of the "religious" when she described the emotion that came with "the great awakening of social consciousness in the labor movement."[39] It is a feeling of connectedness, emanating from the "realization of values that inhere in the actual connections of human beings with one another." But in the case of religion, as in art, its institutionalized form is fraught with sectarianism and hierarchies. Rather, as Dewey wrote, "All modes of human association are 'affected with a public interest,' and full realization of this interest is equivalent to a sense of a significance that is religious in its function." Thus, "to segregate the implicit public interest and social value of all institutions and social arrangements in a particular organization," such as a certain sect or specific church, "is a fatal diversion." Instead let us harness "intelligence as a force in social action," with "devotion, so intense as to be religious,"[40] Dewey secularly proclaimed.

By the time Dewey wrote the introduction to his 1946 edition of *The Public and Its Problems*, twenty years after its first publication,[41] he admitted that putting faith only in scientific method applied to social affairs was not the answer, as "exhibited in what has followed upon the fission of the atom."[42] The consequences of science, like politics — or life for that matter — always present us with moral issues. As a democratic society, moral principles need to be made common, continually reaffirmed, and re-embodied through communication. Democracy itself is that means: "For what is the faith of democracy in the method of consultation, of conference, of persuasion, of discussion, in forming of public opinion, which in the long run is self-corrective, except faith in the capacity of the intelligence of the common man to respond with common sense to the free play of facts and ideas which are secured by effective guarantees of free inquiry, free assembly and free communication?"[43]

Democracy, Dewey knew, requires intelligent communication to make change. "There is such a thing as passionate intelligence,"[44] he wrote, hopefully, that drives us to do what we care about and believe in. This has existed throughout history. While he admitted being dismissed as utopian in his belief in intelligence,[45] he remained committed to intelligent human progress.[46]

Putting faith in intelligence, Dewey looked to expand the acquisition of knowledge through the social as well as natural sciences.[47] Certainly experts would play their part, but the public needed to develop the ability to judge information based on common concerns.[48] But for this to occur, we have to recognize that "the notion that intelligence is a personal endowment or personal attainment is the great conceit of the intellectual class, as that of the commercial class is that wealth is something which they personally have wrought and possess." Seeking to recalibrate intelligence and our stake in it, Dewey desired to educate a better-informed public that could act consciously. "The essential need, in other words, is the improvement of the methods and conditions of debate, discussion and persuasion. That is *the* problem of the public."[49]

Thus, he advocated that public education was essential to a democratic society. His brand of education — what we now call critical thinking — was directed to training a "habit of discriminating inquiry and discriminating belief, the ability to look beneath a floating surface to detect the conditions that fix the contour of the surface, and the forces which create its waves and drifts." An educated, discriminating mind would cultivate a "habit of suspended judgment, of skepticism, of desire for evidence, of appeal to observation rather than sentiment, discussion rather than bias, inquiry rather than conventional idealizations." Motivated and slyly mischievous, he concluded: "When this happens, schools will be dangerous outposts of a humane civilization. But they will also begin to be supremely interesting places. For it will then have come about that education and politics are one and the same thing, because politics will have to be in fact what it now pretends to be, the intelligent management of social affairs."[50]

For Dewey, education must include the arts to assure critical thinking, even as leaders during his times (and ours) tried to strip away the arts, fearing therein that sharpening the critical potential of each human being runs the risk of greater class mobility.[51] But Dewey stood by his devotion to the arts, which not only facilitated a discriminating mind but also was just what he thought was needed for all of us to be as artists in our own vocation: to live life as a continual act of creation, conscious and caring about the consequences of our actions. Art school training is but one path, because we all have access to living our lives as works of art if we listen to what gives us energy, what makes us grow and feel alive, and heed what drains our energy away. Taking risks as we practice openness, insights emerge as we live life as a process, learning from what it teaches us along the way, sensing more clearly what matters to us, the values we hold, how the world affects us, and what effect we might have on it. Drawing upon the known and the unknown, we employ intelligence to go forward.

Still, the road is neither fixed nor fully delineated; it goes in and out of clarity, taking turns by our own volition or through circumstances beyond our control. We can act, nonetheless, using and contributing our intelligence, when we become conscious of our place in a continuously evolving human community. So Dewey advised we "accept life and experience in all its uncertainty, mystery, doubt, and half knowledge and turn that experience upon itself to deepen and intensify its own qualities — turn to imagination and art."[52]

John Dewey had a creative, lifelong practice, living his life as art. It was how he practiced democracy, too. And in living his art, he believed he could make a more meaningful life for himself and for others.

Notes

Introduction

1. Dewey's passing in and out of American consciousness was remarked upon even in the twenties when Waldo Frank wrote in the *New Yorker*: "You have probably heard of him—vaguely. You have probably read some of his essays, and not quite gathered what they are about.... No matter... He has influenced *you*. He is the most influential American alive." Waldo Frank, "The Man Who Made Us What We Are," *New Yorker*, May 22, 1926, 15.

2. See John Dewey, "Presenting Thomas Jefferson," in *The Living Thoughts of Thomas Jefferson* (New York: Longmans, Green, 1940).

3. See Jay Martin, *The Education of John Dewey: A Biography* (New York: Columbia University Press, 2002): 165–68.

4. See Mary Jane Jacob, *In Reflections on Evoking History: Listening across Cultures and Communities.* Charleston, SC: Spoleto Festival USA, 2001.

5. See Mary Jane Jacob, Michael Brenson, and Eva Olson, *Culture in Action: New Public Art in Chicago* (Seattle: Bay Press, 1995) and Joshua Decter, Helmut Drexler, et al, *Exhibition as Social Intervention: "Culture in Action"* (London: St. Martin's Press, Afterall Books, Exhibition Histories series, 2014).

6. See Mary Jane Jacob and Michael Brenson, *Conversations at the Castle: Changing Audiences and Contemporary Art* (Cambridge: MIT Press, 1998).

7. Jacquelynn Baas and Mary Jane Jacob, eds., *Buddha Mind in Contemporary Art* (Berkeley: University of California Press, 2004).

8. This led to the essay "Like Minded: Jane Addams, John Dewey, and László Moholy-Nagy," in *Chicago Makes Modern*, which I coedited with Jacquelynn Baas (Chicago: University of Chicago Press, 2012).

9. Mary Jane Jacob and Kate Zeller, eds., Chicago Social Practice History Series: *Art Against the Law, Immersive Life Practices, Institutions and Imaginaries, A Lived Practice*, and *Support Networks* (Chicago: School of the Art Institute of Chicago, 2014–15).

Chapter 1

1. John Dewey, quoted in *Dialogue on John Dewey*, ed. Corliss Lamont (New York: Horizon Press, 1959), 95.

2. John Dewey, *Art as Experience* (New York: Penguin, [1934] 2005), 222.

3. John Dewey, *Experience and Nature* (New York: Dover Publications, [1925] 1958), 378.

4. Dewey's use of the term "mechanic" was not restricted to one who repairs a vehicle or other machine, though Robert Pirsig draws on this common usage today to identify his fictional characters. In Dewey's time, it referred to a range of skilled manual labor. During the nineteenth-century Industrial Revolution, Mechanics' Institutes were educational institutions that offered technical skills as well as recreation. The movement began in Scotland and spread worldwide.

5. Dewey, *Art as Experience*, 4.

6. Robert M. Pirsig, *Zen and the Art of Motorcycle Maintenance: An Inquiry into Values* (New York: Harper Collins, 1974), 34.

7. Pirsig, 281.

8. Pirsig, 275. While Pirsig never mentions Dewey, Granger went on to investigate the deep thematic parallels. See David A. Granger, *John Dewey, Robert Pirsig, and the Art of Living* (New York: Palgrave Macmillan, 2006).

9. John Dewey, *Outlines of a Critical Theory of Ethics* (Ann Arbor, MI: Register, 1891), 169.

10. Pirsig, 111.

11. Artist Conversation: Martin Puryear and Theaster Gates, February 4, 2016, Art Institute of Chicago. https://www.youtube.com/watch?v=_LVmdOrC91c.

12. Dewey, *Art as Experience*, 14.

13. Dewey, 273. Dewey had added in speaking of well-made articles in daily life: "I do not think anyone would suppose that act of use is such as to be anesthetic."

14. Dewey, 357.

15. Peter Korn, *Why We Make Things and Why It Matters: The Education of a Craftsman* (London: Square Peg, Vintage Books, 2013), 152.

16. Katie Paterson, interview by the author, February 3–5, 2016.

17. Pirsig, 296.

18. Dewey, *Art as Experience*, 41. Richard Sennett also channels John Dewey in his book *The Craftsman* when he writes: "Craftsmanship names an enduring, basic

human impulse, the desire to do a job well for its own sake. Craftsmanship cuts a far wider swath than skilled manual labor; it serves the computer programmer, the doctor, and the artist; parenting improves when it is practiced as a skilled craft, as does citizenship." In the conclusion of his book, he acknowledges the role of pragmatism and of Dewey in the development of his argument that "the craft of making physical things provides insight into the techniques of experience that can shape our dealings with others." Richard Sennett, *The Craftsman* (New Haven, CT: Yale University Press, 2008), 9, 289.

19. Korn, 166.

20. Dewey expressed his contempt for what he called the "aloofness" of intellectuals when he wrote: "The ingratitude displayed by thinkers to artists who by creation of harmoniously composed objects supplied idealistic philosophy with empirical models of their ultimately real objects, was shown in even greater measure to artisans. The accumulated results of the observations and procedures of farmers, navigators, builders furnished matter-of-fact information about natural events, and also supplied the pattern of logical and metaphysical subordination of change to directly possessed and enjoyed fulfillments. While thinkers condemned the industrial class and despised labor, they borrowed from them the facts and the conceptions that gave form and substance to their own theories. For apart from processes of art there was no basis for introducing the idea of fulfillment, realization, into the notion of end nor for interpreting antecedent operations as potentialities." Dewey, *Experience and Nature,* 124–25.

21. John Dewey, "Preoccupation with the Disconnected," talk given by Dewey to the New York Academy of Medicine, 1928. First published in and cited here as "Body and Mind," *Bulletin of the New York Academy of Medicine* IV, no. 1 (1928): 8.

22. J. Morgan Puett, interview by the author, May 20, 2013.

23. John Dewey, "Individuality and Experience," *Journal of the Barnes Foundation* 2 (January 1926): 2–3.

24. In the preface to her book *On Weaving*, Albers expressed the feeling of making, the sense of being at the inception of an exploration of timeworn subjects that nonetheless can open out to new worlds, when she wrote:

> Though I am dealing in this book with long-established facts and processes, still, in exploring them, I feel on new ground. And just as it is possible to go from any place to any other, so also, starting from a defined and specialized field, one can arrive at a realization of ever-extending relationships.
>
> Thus tangential subjects come into view. The thoughts, however, can, I believe, be traced to the event of a thread.

Anni Albers, *On Weaving* (Middletown, CT: Wesleyan University Press, 1965): 15. See also Mary Jane Jacob, "Anni Albers: A Modern Weaver as Artist," in *The Woven and Graphic Art of Anni Albers* (Washington, DC: Smithsonian Institution Press, 1985).

25. Thomas Hirschhorn in conversation with Yasmil Raymond, University of Chicago, October 27, 2016.

26. Mary Jane Jacob, "Outside the Loop," in *Culture in Action: New Public Art in Chicago*, by Mary Jane Jacob, Michael Brenson, and Eva M. Olson (Seattle: Bay Press, 1995), 59. Joining Suzanne Lacy's project to define a "new genre public art," as this artist came to call it, I also wrote about how working outside the rarified confines of museums was met with suspicion by the art establishment: "If locally appreciated (on the street level, if you will), such public art works must not be of interest to those situated geographically and socially outside, and the art must lack universality, must not be of aesthetic significance. . . . Its offenses are its connectedness to the actual (not just artifice); its practical function (not just aesthetic experience); its transitory or temporary nature (rather than permanence and collectibility); its public aims and issues as well as public location; its inclusiveness (reaching beyond the predefined museum-going audience); and its involvement of others as active viewers, participants, coauthors, or owners. Moreover, because so many artists have felt the urgency to work this way in the face of the critical needs of our cities and communities, this community responsive, audience-directed work is put down for being trendy, 'dogooder,' and opportunistic, taking advantage of funds created out of new governmental or foundation agendas." Mary Jane Jacob, "An Unfashionable Audience," in *Mapping the Terrain: New Genre Public Art*, ed. Suzanne Lacy (Seattle: Bay Press, 1995), 56.

27. Dewey, *Art as Experience*, 7.

28. Dewey, *Experience and Nature*, 364.

29. Dewey, *Art as Experience*, 1.

30. Dewey, 237–38.

31. Dewey, 4.

32. Dewey said to the press: "I hope all those who are skeptical about the aesthetic possibilities of machine production will see the Exhibition. To my mind there is convincing proof that there is no essential opposition between production for utility and for beauty." The propeller he selected was manufactured by the Aluminum Company of America, Pittsburgh (Alcoa). Press release, Museum of Modern Art, New York, March 5, 1934.

33. Arthur C. Danto, "Museums and the Thirsting Millions," in *After the End of Art: Contemporary Art and the Pale of History* (Princeton, NJ: Princeton University Press, 1997), 179–81.

34. The thought in full was offered in 1938 when speaking to the Dance Association. Dewey said: "Unfortunately, there is a tendency when we think of works of art primarily to associate them with the art museums, the art galleries, or the music hall or opera house, places where we can go and see or hear those objects which

have become recognized as works of art. If we approach the matter from our end we get a more flexible approach and one that is more inclusive, one that is more tolerant. It recognizes that we may have this experience in the presence of all kinds of things — the graciousness of a person in approach and intercourse in relation to other people — that great deeds of people not merely of those who are recognized as heroes, but humble people, may then have the grace or nobility because of the way that they strike us. If we approach from this side it seems to me that it tends to enlarge us. If we become more on the lookout for the moments of this kind of experience we do not think of them as experiences we have to have by going to certain places, but that we may have at any time of day in connection with any, not everyone, but with contacts with objects, scenes, persons that are not in any way labeled to be works of fine art." Not previously published, from a transcript of a lecture delivered November 13, 1938, to the Washington Dance Association at the Phillips Memorial Gallery, Washington, DC. Transcript in Fletcher Free Library, Burlington, VT. Cited in *John Dewey: The Later Works, 1925–1953*, vol. 13: *1938–39, Essays, Experience and Education, Freedom and Culture, The Theory of Valuation*, ed. Jo Ann Boydston (Carbondale: Southern Illinois University, [1984] 2003), 359.

35. Dewey, *Art as Experience*, 2, 9.

36. Francis V. O'Conner, ed., *Art for the Millions: Essays from the 1930s by Artists and Administrators of the WPA Federal Art Project* (Boston: New York Graphic Society, 1975), 33.

37. O'Conner, 36, 44.

38. Dewey, *Art as Experience*, 339.

39. O'Conner, 35.

40. O'Conner, 36.

41. O'Conner, 35.

42. Holger Cahill, *New Horizons in American Art* (New York: Museum of Modern Art, 1936), 18.

43. O'Conner, *Art for the Millions*, 40.

44. Both identities of artists are probed by Michael Brenson in his important treatise, which emerged from the Culture Wars and the political Right's expunging of artists from the federal budget as a call to cleanse America's morality. See Michael Brenson, *Visionaries and Outcasts: The NEA, Congress, and the Place of the Visual Artist in America* (New York: New Press, 2001).

45. Cahill, 16.

46. O'Conner, 37.

47. The Index of American Design is housed at the National Gallery of Art, Washington, DC, and is also available on line: http://www.nga.gov/collection/gallery/iad.htm.

48. Cahill, 21–22.

49. This can be mapped from Old Sturbridge Village in Massachusetts, incorpo-

rated in 1935 and whose founding is attributed to the influence of Dewey's ideas, to the Dakota Discovery Museum in Mitchell, South Dakota, for which the philosopher was a signing supporter in 1939. These public efforts stand in contrast to private ventures to construct images of American culture by John D. Rockefeller Jr. at Colonial Williamsburg, Virginia, beginning in 1926, and Henry Ford's Greenfield Village in Dearborn, Michigan, in 1933.

50. Some centers evolved into more established museums, like the Des Moines Art Center, Phoenix Art Museum, and Walker Art Center (formerly Minneapolis Community Art Center); others have become active contemporary art Kunsthalle with robust education programs like Chicago's Hyde Park Art Center; while some struggle to hold on to collections like Southside Community Arts Center, Chicago.

51. See John Dewey, *Freedom and Culture* (New York: G. P. Putnam's Sons, 1939).

52. John Dewey, "Art as Our Heritage," *Congressional Record*, 76th Cong., 3d sess., April 29, 1940, 86, pt. 2477–78, from an April 25 radio address over WMAI, Washington, DC.

53. Brenson, 1.

54. Brenson, 91.

55. Brenson, 91.

56. The strategic use of federal funds in the 1970s through the Comprehensive Employment and Training Act (CETA) aided artists but was short lived.

57. Brenson, 157. I built my curatorial foundation on these same questions, as I felt the need to flee the graduate-school canon of art history in the seventies. I first took up the subject of the art of the Shakers, pairing it with the work of early modernist American artist Charles Sheeler. In my first museum post as a curator at the Detroit Institute of Arts, I brought to light Sheeler's 1927 Ford River Rouge Plant as an experiment in the "low" art of photography and advertising that complemented his engagement of the "high" art of painting, with both serving as terrain on which he played out his search for an American subject that spoke to the culture of his own time. I also became dedicated to exposing the work of local artists (so-called art outside the mainstream, as Marcia Tucker dubbed it), first in Detroit and then in Chicago, all the while taking to heart lessons learned during a Cahill-like internship with the Michigan Council for the Arts Artrain that brought art to people across the nation.

Chapter 2

1. Rirkrit Tiravanija, conversation with the author, April 26, 2014.

2. Brian Andrews and Patricia Maloney, "Episode 487: Rick Lowe," from *Bad at Sports: Contemporary Art Talk*, December 29, 2014. http://badatsports.com/2014/episode-487-rick-lowe/.

3. Akin to the way the writing of theory was but one half of an equation that must be fulfilled in practice, Dewey wrote of the inadequacy of language to express the emotion that occurs within experience but which can be captured in the making of art: "The notion that expression is a direct emission of an emotion complete in itself entails logically that individualization is specious and external. . . . Were this idea correct, works of art would necessarily fall within certain types. . . . The unique, unduplicated character of experienced events and situations impregnates the emotion that is evoked. Were it the function of speech to reproduce that to which it refers . . . [a] lifetime would be too short to reproduce in words a single emotion. . . . Instead of a description of an emotion in intellectual and symbolic terms, the artist 'does the deed that breeds' the emotion." John Dewey, *Art as Experience* (New York: Penguin, [1934] 2005), 70.

4. Dewey, *Art as Experience*, 37–38.

5. Dewey, *Reconstruction of Philosophy* (New York: Henry Holt, 1920), 91.

6. John Dewey, *The Quest for Certainty: A Study of the Relation of Knowledge and Action* (New York: G. P. Putnam's Sons, 1929), 146.

7. Dewey, *Art as Experience*, 36–37.

8. Dewey, 339, 50.

9. John Dewey, "Aesthetic Experience as a Primary Phase and as an Artistic Development," *Journal of Aesthetics and Art Criticism* 9, no. 1 (September 1950): 56, 57.

10. Dewey, *Art as Experience*, 309.

11. Dewey, 344, 1.

12. Jeon Joonho, *About Beauty*, video, 2013.

13. Dewey, *Experience and Nature* (New York: Dover Publications, [1925] 1958), 389.

14. Dewey, *Art as Experience*, 9, 10.

15. Dewey, "Aesthetic Experience as a Primary Phase," 57.

16. Dewey, *Art as Experience*, 3.

17. Dewey, 113, 344, 113.

18. By contrast, Claire Bishop would have us believe that if we are not direct participant-collaborators, that is, on site at the moment, we remain outside the experience, doomed to be a secondary audience, as she calls it. She writes: "By using people as a medium, participatory art has always had a double ontological status: it is both an event in the world, and also at a remove from it. As such, it has the capacity to communicate on two levels—to participants and to spectators—the paradoxes that are repressed in everyday discourse, and to elicit perverse, disturbing, and pleasurable experiences that enlarge our capacity to imagine the world and our relations anew. But to reach the second level requires a mediating third term—an object, image, story, film, even a spectacle—that permits this experience to have a purchase on the public imaginary." Claire Bishop, "Participation and Spectacle: Where We Are

Now?" in *Living As Form: Socially Engaged Art from 1991–2011*, ed. Nato Thompson (Cambridge, MA: MIT Press and Creative Time, 2012), 45.

19. Dewey, *Art as Experience*, 339. Joshua Decter applied this to socially engaged art practice: "Art is social even when it claims — or appears — to be turning away from the social. . . . If art is *always* socially constructed, then art that understands itself as being *socially engaged* transmits a particular desire to connect into broader constituencies, with potentially distinct values and interests. In other words, a demotic conception of art is envisaged: a repositioning or redistributing of art into the social demos. Participatory and collaborative art practice reflects an amplification and elevation of post-individual (or post-autonomous), group-generated and collectively iterated procedures; these seem more social because they appear to be more directly the product of scaled-up socialised processes *vis-à-vis* autonomous art-making — which, of course, is never fully autonomous, given the elaborately interpersonal network of production, display and socialising that is embedded within art practice. Art is intrinsically biosocial and biopolitical." Joshua Decter, "Culture in Action: Exhibition as Social Redistribution," in *Exhibition as Social Intervention: "Culture in Action" 1993*, ed. Joshua Decter, Helmut Draxler et al. (London: Afterall Books, 2014), 16–17.

20. Dewey, *Art as Experience*, 18, 13.

21. David Brick, "Eiko Otake and the Politics of Hesitation," September 30, 2014. http://headlong.org/eiko-otake-and-the-politics-of-hesitation/.

22. David Brick, correspondence with the author, May 8, 2014.

23. Dewey, *Art as Experience*, 54–55.

24. Dewey, *Experience and Nature*, 371.

25. Allan Kaprow and Jeff Kelley, eds., *Essays on the Blurring of Art and Life* (Berkeley: University of California Press, 1993), xiii.

26. Kaprow and Kelley, xvi. He goes on to cite other instances of Kaprow's close read of Dewey's *Art as Experience* in his introduction.

27. Kaprow and Kelley, xxiv.

28. Kaprow and Kelley, xxiv. Kelley draws a parallel between Zen and Dewey: "Like Dewey's pragmatism, Zen mistrusts dogma and encourages education, seeks enlightenment but avoids formalist logic, accepts the body as well as the mind, and embraces discipline but relinquishes ego-centered control. In establishing discipline as a contemplative practice that opens the practitioner to knowledge, Zen loosely parallels the scientific method, in which controls are established in an experimental process that opens the researcher to phenomena. For Kaprow, pragmatism is the mechanics of Zen, and Zen the spirit of pragmatism. . . . Though the link between Zen and Cagean esthetics is well known in the American arts, it was Dewey's pragmatism that best prepared Kaprow to accept it as method."

29. Eugen Herrigel, *Zen in the Art of Archery* (New York: Vintage Books, Random House, [1953] 1999), 6. Herrigel also offers a Deweyan unity of experience as he writes of learning archery: "In spite of being divided into parts the entire process

seemed like a living thing wholly contained in itself, and not even remotely comparable to a gymnastic exercise, to which bits can be added or taken away without its meaning and character being thereby destroyed" (21).

30. Dewey, *Art as Experience*, 2, 58.

31. Dewey, 302.

32. Dewey, 50.

33. Dewey, 56.

34. Dewey, 348.

35. Dewey, 56.

36. Marcel Duchamp delivered "The Creative Act" as an address to the American Federation of Arts in a session on the creative act at its convention in Houston, Texas, in April 1957. It was first published in essay form in *Art News* 56 (Summer 1957): 28–29.

37. Joseph Beuys was himself influenced by both Eastern thought and Rudolf Steiner.

38. Chögyam Trungpa, "Dharma Art — Genuine Art," in *Dharma Art*, ed. Judith L. Lief (Boston: Shambhala Publications, 1996), 1.

39. In her chapter "Culture in Action" in *One Place after Another* (Cambridge, MA: MIT Press, 2004: 100–137), Miwon Kwon does not reveal any personal experiences and in her framing, dependent on theorists, one would not know that she actually had been a visitor to the sites and a participant in some of the discussions. Since writers rarely divulge their own personal reactions, the question arises as to how much they have really experienced these works, that is, did they have *an* experience. Claire Bishop speaks of the need to be on guard against and not get too close to personal experience; when she cites an experience, it is not via persons unknown to the art world, but rather the reaction to an event as seen through the lens of a celebrity artist she knows (*Artificial Hells: Participatory Art and the Politics of Spectatorship* [London: Verso Press, 2012], 6, 205). Similarly, Hal Foster looks to the learned and intellectual aspects of art but not its embodiment, decidedly eschewing the emotive. In seeking to expose the compromised rather than progressive nature of social practice, he looks for villains among curators, condemning site-specific work as being used for economic development, social outreach, and art tourism (see *The Return of the Real: The Avant-Garde at the End of the Century* [Cambridge, MA: MIT Press, 1996], 197–98). For example, after reading through didactic materials and press releases for *Culture in Action*, he draws the conclusion that this program served the marketing ambitions of the corporations and agencies that supported it, mistaking funding credits for a public relations campaign. To an academic like Foster (whose affiliated institutions of Cornell and Princeton cloak the interests of the contributors behind the imprimatur of these esteemed universities), this superficial read of the scruffy organizing institution, Sculpture Chicago, indicated to him that it had sold out.

40. Dewey, *Art as Experience*, 17.

41. Dewey, 2.

42. Lisa Le Leuvre, "The Time of an Artwork," in *Katie Paterson* (Newcastle upon Tyne, UK and Bielefeld/Berlin, Germany: Locus+ and Kerber Verlag, 2016), 164.

43. *Places with a Past* met much resistance from founder Gian Carlo Menotti. See Allan Kozinn, "Menotti Gives Spoleto Festival an Ultimatum: They Go or I Go," *New York Times*, May 30, 1991. Online at http://www.nytimes.com/1991/05/30/arts /menotti-gives-spoleto-festival-an-ultimatum-they-go-or-i-go.html. As cited there, "When a member of the board [Beatrice Cummings Mayer] quoted Michael Brenson's favorable review of the exhibition in the *New York Times* on Monday as part of a resolution in support of the curator, Mary Jane Jacob, Mr. Menotti stormed out of the meeting." The continuing saga ultimately resulted in Gian Carlo Menotti's departure from the festival in 1993. See Allan Kozinn, "Menotti Leaves Spoleto U.S.A.," *New York Times*, October 26, 1993, http://www.nytimes.com/1993/10/26/arts /menotti-leaves-spoleto-usa.html?pagewanted=all&src=pm. See also Michael Brenson, "Places with a Past: New Site-Specific Art in Charleston Belongs to Its Place and Time," https://brooklynrail.org/2013/07/criticspage/places-with-a-pastnew-site -specific-art-in-charleston-belongs-to-its-place-and-time.

44. For instance, in *Culture in Action*, the aim was to explore how artists' processes could flow into the social dynamic and have meaning for people outside the art world. Among the misperceptions of this program, Joshua Decter points out, "we should be cautious to apply sustainability as the primary criterion of evaluation here, since this outcome was not a precondition of Jacob's curatorial framework." See Joshua Decter, "Culture in Action Revisited," in *Exhibition as Social Intervention: "Culture in Action" 1993*, ed. Joshua Decter, Helmut Draxler et al. (London: Afterall Books, 2014), 41.

45. Michael Brenson, a trusted colleague who experienced my first entry into Charleston in 1991, described my method a decade later as a way of curating that "value[s] an experience in which the primary gesture is one of personal and collective opening, that can give hope for community and the political." Reflecting further on a community conversation in which he participated in 2001 at the beginning of *Places with a Future*, he asked if it was "an art experience"? There was an agency in it that spoke to him of the Deweyan potential for conscious aesthetic experience: "It seemed to me there was a possibility of really talking, of real dialogue, real communication, among the people who came together in Charleston. There was some point, some space, where all these histories could intersect without erasing any of them." Michael Brenson, "Conversation: February 22, 2002," *Reflections on Evoking History: Listening Across Cultures and Communities* (Charleston, SC: Spoleto Festival USA, 2002), 43–44.

46. One astute observer, cultural historian Barbara Kirshenblatt-Gimblett, wrote: "Embodied memory is what we were privileged to witness." Barbara Kirshenblatt-Gimblett, "Reflection on Spoleto's 'Evoking History,'" *Reflections on*

Evoking History: Listening Across Cultures and Communities (Charleston, SC: Spoleto Festival USA, 2002), 24.

47. Edward Ball et al., "Beyond the Flag: Southern Writers Speak," June 3, 2000, Spoleto Festival USA at The Riviera at Charleston Place, Charleston, SC. See http://www.c-span.org/video/?157725-1/southern-writers-confederate-flag.

48. Kendra Hamilton, email to the author, January 20, 2002.

49. For a discussion of the second decade of artists working with communities in Charleston, in part leading to the US Gullah/Geechee Cultural Heritage Corridor Act, see my essay "Audiences Are People, Too: Social Art Practice as Lived Experience" in *The Blackwell Companion to Public Art*, ed. Cher Krause Knight and Harriet F. Senie (Hoboken, NJ: Wiley-Blackwell, 2016): 251–67.

50. See Mary Jane Jacob, "In the Space of Art," in *Buddha Mind in Contemporary Art*, ed. Jacquelynn Baas and Mary Jane Jacob (Berkeley: University of California Press, 2004), 164–69.

51. Walter Hood, "Defining a Cultural Art Practice: The Speculative and the Practical," Masters of Fine Arts Thesis, School of the Art Institute of Chicago, 2013.

52. National Park Service, accessed March 8, 2015. http://www.nps.gov/guge/learn/management/staffandoffices.htm.

Chapter 3

1. Toyo Ito, "Kamaishi Revival Project," in *News from Nowhere: A Platform for the Future and Introspection of the Present* (Seoul: Workroom Press, 2012), 97.

2. Ito, 103.

3. Ernesto Pujol, email to the author, May 1, 2014.

4. Jo Ann Boydston, "John Dewey and the Alexander Technique," keynote address at the International Congress of Teachers of the Alexander Technique, 1986. http://www.alexandercenter.com/jd/deweyalexanderboydston.html.

5. John Dewey to Joseph Ratner, July 24, 1946, in *Correspondence of John Dewey, 1871–1952*, 4 vols., 3: *1940–1953*: 1946.07.24 (07140). Electronic edition: http://pm.nlx.com.proxy.artic.edu/xtf/view?docId=dewey_c_ii/dewey_c_ii.03.xml;chunk.id=id973327;toc.depth=1;toc.id=id961234a;brand=default.

6. John Dewey, "Introduction," in *Constructive Conscious Control of the Individual*, F. Matthias Alexander (New York: E. P. Dutton, 1923), xxxiii. Dewey also wrote: "In the present state of the world, it is evident that the control we have gained of physical energies, heat, light, electricity, etc., without having first secured control of our use of ourselves is a perilous affair. Without the control of our use of ourselves, our use of other things is blind; it may lead to anything. . . . If there can be developed a technique which will enable individuals really to secure the right use of themselves, then the factor upon which depends the final use of all other forms of energy will be brought under control. Mr. Alexander has evolved this technique." John Dewey,

"Introduction," in *The Use of the Self*, by F. Matthias Alexander (New York: E. P. Dutton, [1932] 1942), xviii, xiii.

7. Dewey, *Experience and Nature* (New York: Dover Publications, [1925] 1958), 296–97.

8. John Dewey, "Preoccupation with the Disconnected," talk given to the New York Academy of Medicine, 1928. First published and cited here as "Body and Mind," *Bulletin of the New York Academy of Medicine* 4, no. 1 (1928), 6–7.

9. John Dewey, "Introduction to *The Use of the Self*," in Frederick Mathias Alexander, *The Use of the Self* (New York: E. P. Dutton, 1923), 10.

10. John Dewey, "As the Chinese Think," *Asia* 22 (January 1922): 9–10. It is not surprising that the Alexander Technique has been compared to Vipassana Buddhism; both practices aim for awareness through conscious orientation of the five physical senses and the "sixth sense" of the mind, hence mindfulness. Vipassana and Alexander Technique are also joined by the key role each gives to teachers: in the Alexander Technique, to sense the state of the muscles of the student and help them become aware of the muscles touched; in Buddhism, for no-mind training. This is of note because Dewey's educational platform is built on a shared, cooperative relationship between teacher and student. See Antony Woods, "The Alexander Technique in Relation to Satipatthana Vipassana," http://www.buddhanet.net/filelib/medbud/alextech.txt.

11. John Dewey to Dewey Children, April 1, 1919, in *Correspondence of John Dewey, 1871–1952*, 4 vols., 2: *1919–1939*: 1919.04.01 (10746). Electronic edition: http://pm.nlx.com.proxy.artic.edu/xtf/view?docId=dewey_c_ii/dewey_c_ii.02.xml;query=I%20think%20it%20is%20much%20better%20than%20most%20of%20our%20inside%20formal%20gymnastics.%20;brand=default;hit.rank=1#rank1. The book that Dewey mentions is E. J. Harrison, *The Fighting Spirit of Japan* (London: W. Foulsham, 1912). He also cited in his letters two other occasions when he observed conscious control. On February 22, 1919, while visiting the Women's University in Tokyo, he saw Samurai women's sword and spear exercises: "The teacher was an old woman of seventy-five as lithe and nimble as a cat—more graceful than any of the girls. . . . I have an enormous respect now for the old etiquette and ceremonies regarded as physical culture. Every movement has to be made perfectly, and it cannot be done without conscious control." And on March 10, while attending a Noh drama, he concluded, "Conscious control was certainly born and bred in Japan." John Dewey to his children, 1919.02.22 (03877); and John Dewey to Sabino Dewey 1919.03.10 (10750), both from *Correspondence of John Dewey, 1871–1952*, 4 vols., 2: *1919–1939*.

12. Dewey, *Art as Experience* (New York: Penguin, [1934] 2005), 350.

13. John Dewey, *Reconstruction in Philosophy* (New York: Henry Holt, 1920), 211.

14. Dewey, *Experience in Nature*, 388–89; punctuation per original.

15. Josef Albers, "Art as Experience," *Progressive Education* 12, no. 6 (October 1935): 392, 393. Dewey was a founder of this journal.

16. In 1959, Robert Rauschenberg included the following statement in the catalog for the landmark exhibition *Sixteen Americans*, organized by the Museum of Modern Art in New York: "Painting relates to both art and life. Neither can be made. (I try to act in that gap between the two.)" Artist's statement in Dorothy C. Miller, ed., *Sixteen Americans* (New York: Museum of Modern Art, 1959), 58. The importance of this statement cannot be underestimated in terms of the intellectual floodgates it opened in the art world of the 1950s, altering the discourse surrounding the age-old question of what is art. http://www.walkerart.org/collections/artists/robert -rauschenberg.

17. This and subsequent quotations from Carolyn Laib, interview by the author, October 20, 2011.

18. Carolyn Laib was initially drawn to her future husband's art because of her own experiences with art as a conservator, perceiving that "a painting can have a kind of energy." As her own career became her practice, she reflected, "to work effectively on a work of art, to care for it, you have to become a part of it. You have to take the time to be one with the energy of whatever it is you're approaching. . . . The ability to treat an object, to take it to some new state, can only happen if you are at one with the energy of that piece." Interview by the author, October 20, 2011.

19. John Dewey, *Reconstruction in Philosophy* (New York: Henry Holt, 1920), 181.

20. Richard Florida, *The Rise of the Creative Class: And How It's Transforming Work, Leisure, Community and Everyday Life* (Cambridge, MA: Basic Books, 2002), 166. Critic Joshua Decter writes: "Today it seems that the liberal humanist, cultural-evangelical notion of art as an agent of urban social change may have been repurposed by closet neoliberals such as Richard Florida, who promotes the notion of a 'creative class' positively impacting the economic, cultural and social redevelopment of cities. Although there may be a ring of truth to this argument, many on the cultural left view it as a pernicious instrumentalisation of art and culture — as a not-so-hidden defence of an urban gentrification process whereby artists often get priced out of the very neighbourhoods they helped to productively transform." Joshua Decter, "Culture in Action Revisited," in *Exhibition as Social Intervention: "Culture in Action" 1993*, ed. Joshua Decter, Helmut Draxler et al. (London: Afterall Books, 2014), 18.

21. Ernesto Pujol, email to the author, March 4, 2015.

22. Ernesto Pujol, email to the author, March 3, 2015.

23. Ernesto Pujol and Thyrza Nichols Goodeve, "Vulnerability as Critical Self-Knowledge," *Brooklyn Rail*, October 3, 2013. http://www.brooklynrail.org/2013/10 /art/vulnerability-as-critical-self-knowledgeernesto-pujol-with-thyrza-nichols -goodeve.

24. See Shunryu Suzuki, *Zen Mind, Beginner's Mind: Informal Talks on Zen Meditation and Practice* (New York: Weatherhill, 1970).

25. Ann Hamilton, *the event of the thread*, artist talk, Park Avenue Armory, New York, December 8, 2013.

26. John Dewey, *Logic: The Theory of Inquiry* (New York: Henry Holt, 1938), 105.

27. Dewey, *Art as Experience*, 13.

28. John Dewey, *Democracy and Education: An Introduction to the Philosophy of Education* (New York and London: Free Press and Collier-Macmillan, [1916] 1944), 146.

29. Dewey said: "Just because a problem well stated is on its way to solution, the determining of a genuine problem is a *progressive* inquiry; the cases in which a problem and its probable solution flash upon an inquirer are cases where much prior ingestion and digestion have occurred. If we assume, prematurely, that the problem involved is definite and clear, subsequent inquiry proceeds on the wrong track." Dewey, *Logic*, 108.

30. John Dewey, "Individuality and Experience," *Journal of the Barnes Foundation* 2 (January 1926): 6.

31. Dewey, *Experience and Nature*, 379.

32. Dewey, *Art as Experience*, 16. Within his own work Dewey recognized that each "successive stage of thinking is a conclusion in which the meaning of what has produced it is condensed; and it is no sooner stated than it is a light radiating to other things." Dewey, *Experience and Nature*, 378.

33. John Dewey, *Experience and Nature*, 373.

34. Claire Bishop wrote of the projects in *Culture in Action*: "On a formal level they are uncertain in their beginnings and endings, and impossible to represent visually through photographic documentation." Failing to perceive that they were trusted, temporary creative processes consciously triggering open cultural processes, she goes on to problematize their outcomes, looking for immediate and demonstrable deliverables. "In terms of a social goal, the projects in 'Culture in Action' are also somewhat contradictory: on the one hand, they express an activist desire to be interacting directly with new audiences and accomplishing concrete goals; on the other, they do this through an embrace of open-endedness, in which the artist is reconfigured as a facilitator of others' creativity." See Claire Bishop, *Artificial Hells: Participatory Art and the Politics of Spectatorship* (London: Verso, 2012), 205. Bishop (like the critic cited in regard to the *We Got It!* candy bar in chap. 2) fails to understand that these artists' projects did not seek to turn people into "new audiences." That is a gallery and museum notion of human recruitment, of securing ticket-buyers and eliciting new memberships. They were about true membership, a membership of meaning in a social context. This served to value the communities with which they were aligned, with the artists becoming temporary members of those communities.

35. Dewey, *Reconstruction in Philosophy*, 177.

36. Eugen Herrigel, *Zen in the Art of Archery* (New York: Vintage Spiritual Classics, 1999): 22, 37–38, 38–39.

37. Mike Cross, "Practicing Detachment: A Short Introduction to the F.M. Alexander Technique for Buddhist Practitioners," http://www.alexandertechnique.com/articles/zen/.

38. This became clearer to me as I co-organized and carried out the research consortium "Awake: Art, Buddhism, and the Dimensions of Consciousness"; the insight led to the publication *Buddha Mind in Contemporary Art*, ed. Jacquelynn Baas and Mary Jane Jacob (Berkeley: University of California Press, 2004).

39. Katie Paterson, interview by the author, February 3–5, 2016.

40. Paterson.

41. Chögyam Trungpa, "Art in Everyday Life," in *Dharma Art*, ed. Judith L. Lief (Boston: Shambhala Publications, 1996), 27.

Chapter 4

1. John Dewey, "Democracy Is Radical," *Common Sense* 6 (January 1937): 10–11.

2. Marc Fischer, *Against Competition* (Chicago: Temporary Services, 2014), 4.

3. Daniel Martinez, email to the author and Michael Brenson, January 4, 2014.

4. John Dewey, *Individualism Old and New* (New York: Minton, Balch, 1930), 77.

5. John Dewey, *Liberalism and Social Action* (New York: G. P. Putnam's Sons, 1935), 39.

6. Daniel Martinez, email to the author and Michael Brenson, January 4, 2014.

7. Tania Bruguera from "Commencement Speech," School of the Art Institute of Chicago, May 16, 2016.

8. Fischer, *Against Competition*, 9.

9. John Dewey, *Democracy and Education: An Introduction to the Philosophy of Education* (New York: Free Press and Collier-Macmillan [1916], 1944), 356.

10. John Dewey, *Reconstruction in Philosophy* (New York: Henry Holt, 1920), 122, 121.

11. John Dewey, "John Dewey," in *Living Philosophies*, by Albert Einstein et al. (New York: Simon and Schuster, 1931), 25.

12. John Dewey, "Progress," *International Journal of Ethics* 26 (April 1916): 312.

13. John Dewey, "The Future of Liberalism," *Journal of Philosophy* 32 (April 1935): 228. Originally delivered as an address to the 24th annual meeting of the American Philosophical Association on December 28, 1934 and then published in the journal *School and Society*, January 19, 1935.

14. Dewey, "Progress," 312.

15. Dewey, 313, 315.

16. Dewey, *Reconstruction in Philosophy*, 209–10.

17. John Dewey, "Creative Democracy — The Task Before Us," *John Dewey and*

the Promise of America, Progressive Education Booklet No. 14 (Columbus, OH: American Education Press, 1939): 16, 17.

18. Saul Alinsky would take up the word "radical" in his two books: *Reveille for Radicals* (Chicago: University of Chicago Press, 1946) and *Rules for Radicals: A Pragmatic Primer for Realistic Radicals* (New York: Random House, 1971). As a student in sociology at the University of Chicago (1926–32), he would have been exposed to Dewey's texts, as they were part of its foundation. See Lawrence J. Engel, "Saul D. Alinsky and the Chicago School," *Journal of Speculative Philosophy* 16, no. 1 (2002): 50–66. This can be seen in the idea that human nature has a dual aspect, both individual and social, that the search for community is a modern condition, and that democracy is a radical form of government evolving: "Alinsky's belief and devotion [are] radical; democracy is still a radical idea in a world where we often confuse images with realities, words with actions" (Hillary D. Rodham, "There Is Only the Fight": An Analysis of the Alinsky Model" (bachelor's thesis, Wellesley College, Wellesley, MA, 1969), 10–11, 68–69; quotation at 11.

19. Dewey, "Creative Democracy," 13.

20. Dewey, *Reconstruction in Philosophy*, 194.

21. Dewey, "Creative Democracy," 16.

22. Dewey, 14.

23. Dewey, *Liberalism and Social Action*, 39.

24. See John Dewey, *Individualism Old and New* (New York: Minton, Balch, 1930) and John Dewey, *Liberalism and Social Action*. The latter was fittingly dedicated to the "memory of Jane Addams," who had died in Chicago that year.

25. Dewey, *Liberalism and Social Action*, 34, 39.

26. Dewey, *Freedom and Culture* (New York: G. P. Putnam's Sons, 1939), 22–23.

27. Dewey, *The Public and Its Problems* (New York: Henry Holt, 1927) 193–94.

28. John Dewey, *Freedom and Culture*, 59.

29. Dewey, *Liberalism and Social Action*, 67.

30. Dewey, 69. Speaking of the social character of intelligence, Dewey also recalls the example of nineteenth-century American political economist Henry George, who wrote that the better quality of shipbuilding in his day was "not an improvement of human nature; it is an improvement of society—it is due to a wider and fuller union of individual efforts in accomplishment of common ends." Dewey, *Liberalism and Social Action*, 68.

31. "You didn't build that," *Wikipedia: The Free Encyclopedia*. https://en.wiki pedia.org/wiki/You_didn%27t_build_that.

32. Dewey, *A Common Faith* (New Haven, CT: Yale University Press, 1934), 87.

33. Dewey, *Liberalism and Social Action*, 65.

34. Moreover, Dewey wrote: "Only by participating in the common intelligence and sharing in the common purpose as it works for the common good can individual

human beings realize their true individualities and become truly free" (*Liberalism and Social Action*, 25).

35. Dewey, *The Public and Its Problems*, 149.

36. John Dewey, "Presenting Thomas Jefferson," in *The Living Thoughts of Thomas Jefferson* (New York: Longmans, Green, 1940), 15.

37. Lewis Hyde, "The Common Self," in *A Lived Practice*, Chicago Social Practice History Series (Chicago: School of the Art Institute of Chicago, 2015), 90.

38. See Hyde, "Common Self," and also Lewis Hyde, *Common as Air: Revolution, Art, and Ownership* (New York: Farrar, Straus and Giroux, 2010).

39. Hyde, "The Common Self," 90.

40. Steven Durland, "Looking for Art in the Process," in *Conversations at the Castle: Changing Audiences and Contemporary Art*, ed. Mary Jane Jacob and Michael Brenson (Cambridge, MA: MIT Press, 1998), 146.

41. John Dewey, *Outlines of a Critical Theory of Ethics* (Ann Arbor, MI: Register, 1891), 150.

42. Dewey, *Freedom and Culture*, 21. At about the same time Dewey was writing his major texts on democracy, he contributed a brief introduction to a volume on Vedic philosophy, though he dissuades anyone from taking him to be an authority on the subject. See John Dewey, "Introduction," Jagadish Chandra Chatterji, *India's Outlook on Life: The Wisdom of the Vedas* (New York: Kailas Press, 1931). In the opening pages of the book Chatterji presents the concept of the ultimate Self, timeless and greater than ourselves: "we have the direct experience, however vague, of this Being in the uttermost depths of our existence: we feel that we *are*." He goes on to say that this is not the mind, or soul, or spirit, as in the English language, but can only really be known through experience, a function of awareness (15). This was not the first time Dewey was exposed to Asian thought. Notable is his frequent publisher Paul Carus's enthusiasm for Asian thought and employment of Daisetsu Teitaro Suzuki as a translator in LaSalle, Illinois, beginning in 1897 while Dewey was in nearby Chicago. When Dewey visited Japan in 1919 he reunited with Suzuki. He then went on for an extended stay in China; later he became the sponsor for Asian students at Columbia University and for a time became known as the only major American philosopher interested in Asian philosophy. See Jay Martin, *The Education of John Dewey: A Biography* (New York: Columbia University Press, 2002), 311.

43. Hyde, "Common Self," 88.

44. "When Indra fashioned the world, he made it as a web, and at every knot in the web is tied a pearl. Everything that exists, or has ever existed, every idea that can be thought about is a pearl in Indra's net. Not only is every pearl tied to every other pearl by virtue of the web on which they hang, but on the surface of every pearl is reflected every other jewel on the net. Everything that exists in Indra's web implies all else that exists." Timothy Brook, *Vermeer's Hat: The Seventeenth Century and the Dawn of the Global World* (London: Profile Books, 2008), 22.

45. Hyde, "Common Self," 94.

46. Dewey, *Freedom and Culture*, 9.

47. Magdalena Abakanowicz, *Fate and Art: Monologue* (Milan: Skira, 2008), 153.

48. Dewey, *Art as Experience* (New York: Penguin, [1934] 2005), 360.

49. See Alfredo Jaar, *A Hundred Times Nguyen* (Stockholm: Fotografiska Museet in Moderna Museet, 1994).

50. Alfredo Jaar, "It Is Difficult," in *Learning Mind: Experience Into Art*, ed. Jacquelynn Baas and Mary Jane Jacob, (Berkeley: University of California Press, 2009), 84.

51. Jaar, 84, 88.

52. Tania Bruguera, "Citizen Manifesto for European Democracy, Solidarity, and Equality," *Manifestos*. http://www.taniabruguera.com/cms/676-0-Citizens +Manifesto+for+European+Democracy+Solidarity+and+Equality.htm.

53. This and subsequent quotes from an interview with Tania Bruguera by Pablo Helguera and Mary Jane Jacob, November 15, 2012.

54. Tania Bruguera, "Arte Útil," *Glossary*. http://www.taniabruguera.com/cms /609-0-.htm.

55. Tania Bruguera, "Commencement Speech," School of the Art Institute of Chicago, May 16, 2016.

56. Dewey, *Freedom and Culture*, 10.

57. Dewey, *The Public and Its Problems*, 153.

58. Dewey, 154.

59. Dewey recognized this from the time of his early philosophical writings, as he took up the relation of self to others and to the world. Writing of the moral value of science and art, he said: "It is because through them [that] wants are interconnected, unified and socialized, that they are, when all is said and done, the preeminent moral means." To this he added, already keenly aware that the power of art as an agent of change was under threat and, thus, contained so as to be removed from daily life: "If we do not readily recognize [the arts] in this garb, it is because we have made of them such fixed things, that is, such abstractions, by placing them outside the movement of human life." John Dewey, *Outlines of a Critical Theory of Ethics* (Ann Arbor, MI: Register, 1891), 237–38.

60. My thanks for this phrase, said in conversation with Alexander Robins, December 13, 2014. And as Robins wrote: "The direct experience of fine art, Dewey suggests, leads us to appreciation and the heightened value of other practices, including civic and political activity, thus asserting a theoretical link between appreciating the fine arts and developing oneself into a better citizen overall. In this move, Dewey ties the vibrancy of democracy to the concept of 'appreciation'" (Alexander Robins, "Aesthetic Experience and Art Appreciation: A Pragmatic Account" [Atlanta: Emory University, 2015], 19).

61. Zachary Kamin, "Joan Mitchell's *The City*," assignment on having an aesthetic experience with a work of art, for my class "Thinking through Social Practice with Dewey," School of the Art Institute of Chicago, summer 2015.

62. Daniel J. Martinez, "'Culture in Action' Revisited: Daniel J. Martinez in conversation with Michael Brenson," in *Exhibition as Social Intervention: "Culture in Action" 1993*, ed. Joshua Decter, Helmut Draxler et al. (London: Afterall Books, 2014), 207–8.

63. I wrote of this distinction in regard to the projects created for *Culture in Action*, in Mary Jane Jacob, Michael Brenson, and Eva Olson, *Culture in Action: New Public Art in Chicago* (Seattle: Bay Press, 1995).

64. Daniel Martinez, email to the author, December 28, 2013.

65. Daniel Martinez, email to the author and Michael Brenson, January 4, 2014.

66. Corliss Lamont, ed., *Dialogue on John Dewey* (New York: Horizon Press, 1959), 88, 90.

67. Dewey, *Art as Experience*, 22. "Experience is the result, the sign, and the reward of that interaction of organism and environment which, when it is carried to the full, is a transformation of interaction into participation and communication."

68. Dewey wrote: "When I think of the conditions under which men and women are living in many foreign countries today, fear of espionage, with danger hanging over the meeting of friends for friendly conversation in private gatherings, I am inclined to believe that the heart and final guarantee of democracy is in free gatherings of neighbors on the street corner to discuss back and forth what is read in uncensored news of the day, and in gatherings of friends in the living rooms of houses and apartments to converse freely with one another. Intolerance, abuse, calling of names because of differences of opinion about religion or politics or business, as well as because of differences of race, color, wealth or degree of culture are treason to the democratic way of life. For everything which bars freedom and fullness of communication sets up barriers which divide human beings into sets and cliques, into antagonistic sects and factions, and the democratic way of life is undermined. Merely legal guarantees of the civil liberties of free belief, free expression, free assembly are of little avail if in daily life freedom of communication, of give and take of ideas, facts, experiences is choked by mutual suspicion, by abuse, by fear and hatred. These things destroy the essential condition of the democratic way of living even more effectually than open coercion which—as the example of totalitarian states proves—is effective only when it succeeds in breeding hate, suspicion, intolerance in the minds of individual human beings." John Dewey, "Creative Democracy," 15.

69. John Dewey, "My Pedagogic Creed," in *School Journal* 54, no. 3 (January 16, 1897): 77–80.

70. John Dewey to Theodore Dreier, July 18, 1940 [1940.07.18 (13269)], in *The Correspondence of John Dewey, 1871–1952*, 4 vols., 3: *1940–1953*. Electronic edition: http://pm.nlx.com.proxy.artic.edu/xtf/view?docId=dewey_c_ii/dewey_c_ii.03

.xml;query=is%20a%20living%20example%20of%20democracy%20in%20action
;brand=default;hit.rank=1#rank1.

71. John Dewey, "Introduction," in *The Dewey School: The Laboratory School of
the University of Chicago, 1896–1903,* by Katherine Camp Mayhew and Anna Camp
Edwards (New York: D. Appleton-Century, 1936), xiii.

72. Dewey, "My Pedagogic Creed," 80.

73. *Mark Dion: Misadventures of a 21st-Century Naturalist* (New Haven, CT:
Institute for Contemporary Art, Boston, in association with Yale University Press,
2017): 97.

74. Ernesto Pujol, "Footnotes to Social Choreography: The Practice of Carrying
and Releasing Human Weight," unpublished text, June 6, 11, 2016.

75. Pujol, "Footnotes to Social Choreography." For a discussion of what was lost
as Dewey's notion of public education took a plunge in the eighties, see Nicholas
Tampio, "In Praise of Dewey," *Aeon,* July 28, 2016. https://aeon.co/essays/dewey
-knew-how-to-teach-democracy-and-we-must-not-forget-it?mc_cid=f997fb7640
&mc_eid=d851070e1a.

76. Pujol, "Footnotes to Social Choreography."

77. Dewey, "Creative Democracy," 13.

Chapter 5

1. Federal Bureau of Investigation, "To whom it may concern," April 29, 1943
[1943.04.29 (16483)], in *Correspondence of John Dewey, 1871–1952,* 4 vols., 3: *1940–
1953.* Electronic edition: http://pm.nlx.com.proxy.artic.edu/xtf/view?docId=dewey
_c_ii/dewey_c_ii.03.xml;query=1943.04.29%20(16483);brand=default;hit.rank
=3#rank3. Spelling and punctuation per original.

2. John Dewey, *Reconstruction in Philosophy* (New York: Henry Holt, 1920),
116–17.

3. Jacques Rancière, "Uses of Democracy," *On the Shores of Politics* (London:
Verso, 1995), 61.

4. Jay Martin, *The Education of John Dewey: A Biography* (New York: Columbia
University Press, 2002), 161.

5. John Dewey to Alice Chipman Dewey, October 9, 1894 [1894.10.09 (00205)],
Correspondence of John Dewey, 1871–1952, 4 vols., 1: *1871–1918.* Electronic edition:
http://pm.nlx.com.proxy.artic.edu/xtf/view?docId=dewey_c_ii/dewey_c_ii.01
.xml;chunk.id=d1e51299;toc.depth=1;toc.id=d1e50669a;brand=default.

6. John Dewey to Alice Chipman Dewey, October 9, 1894.

7. John Dewey, *The Public and Its Problems* (New York: Henry Holt, 1927), 115.

8. John Dewey, "A Critique of American Civilization," *World Tomorrow* 11 (October 1928): 395, 391.

9. Dewey, 393.

10. Jane Addams, "A Function of the Social Settlement," *Annals of the American Academy of Political and Social Science* 13 (May 1899): 34.

11. Addams, 36.

12. Jane Addams, "Hull House, Chicago: An Effort toward Social Democracy," *Forum* 14 (October 1892): 226.

13. Addams, "Hull House," 237.

14. Addams, "Hull House," 227.

15. John Dewey, "Education and Birth Control," *Nation* 11 (January 27, 1932): 112.

16. For more on birth control, see Diane C. Haslett, "Hull House and the Birth Control Movement: An Untold Story," *Affilia* 12, no. 3 (Fall 1997): 261–77.

17. John Dewey, "The Senate Birth Control Bill," *People's Lobby Bulletin* 2 (May 1932): 2.

18. Dewey, *A Common Faith* (New Haven, CT: Yale University Press, 1934), 64.

19. John Dewey, "Urges Tax on Rich to Meet Debts Cut," *New York Times* (January 26, 1931): 18. Also see John Dewey to Franklin D. Roosevelt, April 6, 1933, in *Correspondence of John Dewey, 1871–1952*, 4 vols., 2: *1919–1939*: 1933.04.06 (07689). Electronic edition: http://pm.nlx.com/xtf/view?docId=dewey_c_ii/dewey_c_ii.02 .xml;doc.view=print;chunk.id=id952570;toc.depth=1;toc.id=id951615a.

20. John Dewey to Franklin D. Roosevelt, March 8, 1933, in *Correspondence of John Dewey, 1871–1952*, 4 vols., 2: *1919–1939*: 1933.03.08 (07653). Electronic edition: http://pm.nlx.com/xtf/view?docId=dewey_c_ii/dewey_c_ii.02.xml;chunk.id=id 947790;toc.depth=1;toc.id=id946629a;brand=default;query=07653#07653.

21. See John Dewey, "Prospects for a Third Party," *New Republic* 71 (July 27, 1931): 278–80.

22. Addams, "Hull House," 226.

23. Addams, "A Function of the Social Settlement," 52.

24. John Dewey to Alice Chipman Dewey, October 9, 1894 [1894.10.09 (00205)], *Correspondence of John Dewey, 1871–1952*, 4 vols., 1: *1871–1918*. Electronic edition: http://pm.nlx.com.proxy.artic.edu/xtf/view?docId=dewey_c_ii/dewey_c _ii.01.xml;chunk.id=d1e51299;toc.depth=1;toc.id=d1e50669a;brand=default.

25. Dewey, *Common Faith*, 27.

26. Morten Goll and Tone Olaf Nielsen, interview by the author, Copenhagen, September 17, 2016.

27. Goll and Nielsen.

28. Addams, "Hull House," 241.

29. Goll and Nielsen.

30. Steven Durland, "Looking for Art in the Process," in *Conversations at the Castle: Changing Audiences and Contemporary Art*, ed. Mary Jane Jacob and Michael Brenson (Cambridge, MA: MIT Press, 1998): 146.

31. Addams, "A Function of the Social Settlement," 36.

32. Dewey, *Art as Experience* (New York: Penguin, [1934] 2005), 339. Dewey wrote, "Esthetic experience is a manifestation, a record and celebration of the life of a civilization, a means of promoting its development, and is also the ultimate judgment upon the quality of a civilization. For while it is produced and is enjoyed by individuals, those individuals are what they are in the content of their experience because of the cultures in which they participate."

33. Corliss Lamont, ed., *Dialogue on John Dewey* (New York: Horizon Press, 1959), 75.

34. John Dewey, "Understanding and Prejudice," in *American Hebrew* 126 (November 29, 1929): 125.

35. Dewey, "Critique of American Civilization," 391.

36. John Dewey, "Democratic Ends Need Democratic Methods for Their Realization," *New Leader* 22 (October 21, 1939): 3.

37. John Dewey, "Future of Liberalism," *School and Society* 41 (January 19, 1935): 74.

38. John Dewey, "Psychology and Justice," *New Republic* (November 23, 1927): 9.

39. Dewey, 9.

40. As Temkin writes in his analysis of the case and its ramifications: "But Dewey reserved perhaps his harshest criticism for the fact that rather than function as a public, extrajudicial committee with the license to examine the case in larger, nonlegalistic perspective and to take into account public opinion, social tensions, class conflict, and the political context of the trial, Lowell and his associates chose instead to simply retry the original case against Sacco and Vanzetti, only this time in secret and without either a jury or the right of cross-examination." And quoting Dewey, the author continues: " 'Although the question at issue is whether there was ground for a new trial, with a new jury, the committee themselves assume the function of a jury in dealing with new evidence so as to deny the new trial.' " Moshik Temkin, *The Sacco-Vanzetti Affair: America on Trial* (New Haven, CT: Yale University Press, 2009), 170.

41. John Dewey, "The Fruits of Nationalism," *World Tomorrow* 10 (1927): 455.

42. John Dewey to Franklin D. Roosevelt, October 22, 1936 [1936.10.22 (19624)], *Correspondence of John Dewey, 1871–1952*, 4 vols., 2: *1919–1939*. Electronic edition: http://pm.nlx.com.proxy.artic.edu/xtf/view?docId=dewey_c_ii/dewey_c_ii.02.xml;chunk.id=id1160520;toc.depth=1;toc.id=;brand=default.

43. James Burnham to Leon Trotsky, April 1, 1937 [1937.04.01 (21566)], *Correspondence of John Dewey, 1871–1952*, 4 vols., 2: *1919–1939*. Electronic edition: http://pm.nlx.com.proxy.artic.edu/xtf/view?docId=dewey_c_ii/dewey_c_ii.02.xml;chunk.id=id1210239;toc.depth=1;toc.id=;brand=default.

44. John Dewey, "To whom it may concern," April 10, 1937 [1937.04.10 (06606)], *Correspondence of John Dewey, 1871–1952*, 4 vols., 2: *1919–1939*. Electronic

edition; http://pm.nlx.com.proxy.artic.edu/xtf/view?docId=dewey_c_ii/dewey_c
_ii.02.xml;chunk.id=id1219310;toc.depth=1;toc.id=;brand=default.

45. See the commission's preliminary report, "Truth Is on the March," first published as a pamphlet (New York: American Committee for the Defense of Leon Trotsky, 1937), 15, from the news release for speech at the Mecca Temple, New York City,
May 9, 1937. Also see the subsequent book *Not Guilty; Report of the Commission of
Inquiry into the Charges Made against Leon Trotsky in the Moscow Trials*, John Dewey,
chairman (New York: Harper and Brothers, 1938).

46. See John Dewey, "Means and Ends, Their Interdependence, and Leon
Trotsky's Essay on 'Their Morals and Ours,'" first published in *New International*
4 (August 1938): 232–33, and Leon Trotsky, "Their Morals and Ours," *New International* (June 1938): 163–73.

47. Martin, 423.

48. John Dewey, "Universal Service as Education," *New Republic* 6 (1916): 309.

49. John Dewey, Francis J. McConnell, and Stephen S. Wise to New York Citizens, under the auspices of the Citizen's Committee on Military Training in New
York Public High Schools [1929.01.18-20 (14746)], *Correspondence of John Dewey,
1871–1952*, 4 vols., 2: *1919–1939*. Electronic edition: http://pm.nlx.com.proxy.artic
.edu/xtf/view?docId=dewey_c_ii/dewey_c_ii.02.xml;chunk.id=id552648;toc
.depth=1;toc.id=;brand=default.

50. Dewey, "Universal Service as Education," 310.

51. John Dewey to Stephen S. Wise [1933.08.12 (06197)], *Correspondence of John
Dewey, 1871–1952*, 4 vols., 2: *1919–1939*. Electronic edition: http://pm.nlx.com.proxy
.artic.edu/xtf/view?docId=dewey_c_ii/dewey_c_ii.02.xml;chunk.id=id972831;toc
.depth=1;toc.id=;brand=default.

52. For a chronology of the history of securing reparations, see Flint Taylor,
"How Activists Won Reparations for the Survivors of Chicago Police Department
Torture: A History of the Movement to Make Chicago Pay for the Crimes of Former
Police Commander Jon Burge," *In These Times*, June 26, 2015. http://inthesetimes
.com/article/18118/jon-burge-torture-reparations.

53. Members of the Chicago Torture Justice Memorials, interview by Rebecca
Zorach, "Justice, Radically Imagined," in *Art Against the Law*, ed. Rebecca Zorach,
Chicago Social Practice History Series, ed. Mary Jane Jacob and Kate Zeller (Chi-
cago: School of the Art Institute of Chicago, 2014), 179.

54. See Erica R. Meiners and Sarah Ross, "'And What Happens to You Concerns
Us Here': Imaginings for a (New) Prison Arts Movement," in *Art Against the Law*,
ed. Rebecca Zorach, Chicago Social Practice History Series, ed. Mary Jane Jacob and
Kate Zeller (Chicago: School of the Art Institute of Chicago, 2014), 17–30.

55. Meiners and Ross, 25.

56. Open-ended inquiry methods of participant-based evaluation can reveal
the richness of lived experiences. For an insightful article on the application of

participant-based evaluation in museums, see Andrew J. Pekarik, "From Knowing to Not Knowing: Moving Beyond 'Outcomes,'" *Curator* 53, no. 1 (January 2010): 105–15.

57. John Dewey, *The Public and Its Problems*, 13, 14.

58. John Cage, *Diary: How to Improve the World (You Will Only Make Matters Worse)*, ed. Joe Biel and Richard Kraft (Catskill, NY: Siglio, 2015), 56.

59. Dewey, *Common Faith*, 81, 53.

60. Some studies have found conservative positions are not in line with these creative values. See Scott Barry Kauffman, "Are Conservatives Less Creative than Liberals," *Psychology Today, Beautiful Minds* blog, November 5, 2008. https://www.psychologytoday.com/blog/beautiful-minds/200811/are-conservatives-less-creative-liberals.

61. Dewey, *Common Faith*, 77.

62. John Dewey, "America in the World," *The Nation* 106 (1918), 287. As just one example, in this essay Dewey states that more than just providing military strength or economic aid, as Americans "we have an idea to contribute, an idea to be taken into account in the world reconstruction after the war." And he notes, "one of the greatest problems which is troubling the old world is that of the rights of nationalities which are included within larger political units. . . . Here, too, the American contribution is radical. We have solved the problem by a completer separation of nationality from citizenship. . . . to us, language, literature, creed, group ways, national culture, are social rather than political, human rather than national interests. Let this idea fly abroad; it bears healing on its wings." He adds, albeit aspirationally since democracy is never done, "In working out to realization the ideas of federation and of the liberation of human interest from political domination we have been, as it were, a laboratory set aside from the rest of the world in which to make, for its benefit, a great social experiment" (287).

63. Dewey, *Common Faith*, 87.

Chapter 6

1. Hari Zayid, "Empathy Won't Save Us in the Fight against Oppression. Here's Why." *Black Girl Dangerous*, August 11, 2015. http://www.blackgirldangerous.org/2015/08/empathy-wont-save-us-in-the-fight-against-oppression-heres-why/.

2. Iñigo Manglano-Ovalle in panel discussion, "Daniel Joseph Martinez in Conversation with Deana Haggag and Iñigo Manglano-Ovalle," April 4, 2017, School of the Art Institute of Chicago, Visiting Artists Program.

3. Lyn Hejinian, *The Language of Inquiry* (Berkeley: University of California Press, 2000), 31.

4. Lyn Hejinian, 31.

5. Lyn Hejinian, 31.

6. Dewey, *Experience and Nature* (New York: Dover Publications, [1925] 1958), 202.

7. John Dewey, *Art as Experience* (New York: Penguin, [1934] 2005), 347–48.

8. Rebecca Lee Reynolds, "Work by Ronald Jones Bears Witness to Emanuel Massacre," *Burnaway*, June 22, 2015. http://burnaway.org/feature/work-by-ronald -jones-bears-witness-to-emanuel-massacre.

9. This Charleston church is located on Calhoun Street, ironically named for slavery's most devoted apologist. President Barack Obama spoke of this church's significance: "Mother Emanuel is, in fact, more than a church. This is a place of worship that was founded by African Americans seeking liberty. This is a church that was burned to the ground because its worshipers worked to end slavery. When there were laws banning all-black church gatherings, they conducted services in secret. When there was a nonviolent movement to bring our country closer in line with our highest ideals, some of our brightest leaders spoke and led marches from this church's steps. This is a sacred place in the history of Charleston and in the history of America." *Washington Post* Staff, "Transcript: Obama Delivers Eulogy for Charleston Pastor, the Rev. Clementa Pinckney," *Washington Post*, June 26, 2015. https://www.washing tonpost.com/news/post-nation/wp/2015/06/26/transcript-obama-delivers -eulogy-for-charleston-pastor-the-rev-clementa-pinckney/?utm_term=.ce6ea5b 971a0. This deed also gave rise to the term "Charleston loophole," a reference to the Charleston shooting and the law allowing federally licensed dealers to sell firearms after a three-day waiting period even if the FBI has not completed its background check.

10. Reynolds, "Work by Ronald Jones."

11. Dewey, *Art as Experience*, 108.

12. Susan Oyama, "Selves and Worlds: Empathy in Context," in *Empathy: Beyond the Horizon*, ed. Marketta Seppälä (Pori, Finland: Pori Art Museum and FRAME Finnish Fund for Art Exchange, 2003), 32, 33.

13. Oyama, 31.

14. John Dewey, "The Unity of the Human Being," in *Intelligence in the Modern World*, ed. Joseph Ratner (New York: Modern Library, 1939), 819–20. Originally published from an address delivered before the College of Physicians in St. Louis, April 21, 1937.

15. Dewey, 821. Dewey's first major contribution on the subject of the unity of man was his influential essay "The Reflex Arc Concept in Psychology," which set out that stimulus and response are not separate, thus replicating the "older dualism of body and soul," but have a "comprehensive, or organic, unity." From *Psychological Review* 3 (July 1896): 357–58.

16. John Dewey, *A Common Faith* (New Haven, CT: Yale University Press, 1934), 19. In another unusually poetic passage, the philosopher explained that "when the emotional force, the mystic force one might say, of communication, of the

miracle of shared life and shared experience is spontaneously felt, the hardness and crudeness of contemporary life will be bathed in the light that never was on land or sea." John Dewey, *Reconstruction in Philosophy* (New York: Henry Holt, 1920), 211.

17. Katie Paterson, interview by the author, February 3–5, 2016.

18. Dewey, *Experience and Nature*, 371.

19. John Dewey to Catherine B. Wurster, April 4, 1949 [1949.04.04 (15121)]. *Correspondence of John Dewey, 1871–1952*, 4 vols., 3: *1940–1953*. Electronic edition: http://pm.nlx.com.proxy.artic.edu/xtf/view?docId=dewey_c_ii/dewey_c_ii.03 .xml;chunk.id=id1510613;toc.depth=1;toc.id=;brand=default.

20. John Dewey to Catherine B. Wurster, April 4, 1949.

21. "The new era of human relationships in which we live is one marked by mass production for remote markets, by cable and telephone, by cheap printing, by railway and steam navigation. Only geographically did Columbus discover a new world. The actual new world has been generated in the last hundred years. . . . Conditions have changed, but every aspect of life, from religion and education to property and trade, shows that nothing approaching a transformation has taken place in ideas and ideals. . . . We have the physical tools of communication as never before. The thoughts and aspirations congruous with them are not communicated, and hence are not common." Dewey, *The Public and Its Problems: An Essay in Political Inquiry* (Chicago: Gateway Books, 1946), 142.

22. Jonathan Franzen, "Sherry Turkle's 'Reclaiming Conversation,'" *New York Times*, September 28, 2015. http://www.nytimes.com/2015/10/04/books/review /jonathan-franzen-reviews-sherry-turkle-reclaiming-conversation.html?_r=0. See also Sherry Turkle, *Reclaiming Conversation: The Power of Talk in a Digital Age* (New York: Penguin Press, 2015).

23. Lauren Cassani Davis, "The Flight from Conversation," *Atlantic*, October 7, 2015. http://www.theatlantic.com/technology/archive/2015/10/reclaiming -conversation-sherry-turkle/409273/.

24. Dewey, *Art as Experience*, 253.

25. Dewey, *The Public and Its Problems*, 211. Dewey attributes the phrase "face-to-face" to pioneering sociologist Charles Horton Cooley, writing on primary groups who addressed questions of communications. C. H. Cooley, *Social Organization: A Study of the Larger Mind* (New York: Charles Scribner's Sons, 1909).

26. Dewey, *The Public and Its Problems*, 154.

27. Michael Brenson, "Conversation," in *Conversations at the Castle: Changing Audiences and Contemporary Art*, ed. Mary Jane Jacob and Michael Brenson (Cambridge, MA: MIT Press, 1998), 121.

28. Brenson, 121–22, 124.

29. Jacquelynn Baas and Mary Jane Jacob, eds., *Buddha Mind in Contemporary Art* (Berkeley: University of California Press, 2004), 190.

30. Michael Brenson, "The Look of the Artist," in *Learning Mind: Experience into*

Art, ed. Jacquelynn Baas and Mary Jane Jacob (Berkeley: University of California Press, 2009), 198.

31. John Dewey, *Democracy and Education: An Introduction to the Philosophy of Education* (New York and London: Free Press and Collier-Macmillan, [1916], 1944), 6.

32. Dewey wrote: "Vision is a spectator; hearing is a participator" (*The Public and Its Problems*, 219).

33. Dewey, *Art as Experience*, 253.

34. Conversations became a part of my practice once I started working outside museums and where the potential for real discussion, unframed by the institution, seemed possible. For instance, this was both the form and content of *Conversations at the Castle* in Atlanta in 1996; the methodology of research and joint inquiry in *Awake: Art, Buddhism, and the Dimensions of Consciousness*, a quarterly national convening in 2001–3 that led to the publication *Buddha Mind in Contemporary Art*; and conversation offered a way of reentering Charleston in 2000 and connecting to a wide range of persons whose stake in this region led to the decade-long project *Places with a Future*.

35. Dewey, *The Public and Its Problems*, 143, 148. He also said: "Wherever there is conjoint activity whose consequences are appreciated as good by all singular persons who take part in it, and where the realization of the good is such as to effect an energetic desire and effort to sustain it in being just because it is a good shared by all, there is in so far a community" (*The Public and Its Problems*, 149).

36. Chantal Mouffe, *The Democratic Paradox* (London: Verso, 2000), 135.

37. Mouffe, 140.

38. Dewey, *Common Faith*, 27.

39. John Dewey to Alice Chipman Dewey, October 9, 1894 [1894.10.09 (00205)], *Correspondence of John Dewey, 1871–1952*, 4 vols., 1: *1871–1918*. Electronic edition: http://pm.nlx.com.proxy.artic.edu/xtf/view?docId=dewey_c_ii/dewey_c_ii.01.xml;chunk.id=d1e51299;toc.depth=1;toc.id=d1e50669a;brand=default. Dewey and Jane Addams's understanding has been misinterpreted as religion at work, and not humanistic. See Grant H. Kester, "Aesthetic Evangelists: Conversion and Empowerment in Contemporary Community Art," *Afterimage* 22 (January 1995): 5–11.

40. Dewey, *Common Faith*, 80, 79.

41. Dewey, *The Public and Its Problems*, iii–xii; originally published by Henry Holt, New York, 1927.

42. Dewey, *The Public and Its Problems* (1946), x.

43. John Dewey, "Creative Democracy — The Task Before Us," *John Dewey and the Promise of America*, Progressive Education Booklet No. 14 (Columbus, OH: American Education Press, 1939), 14–15.

44. Dewey, *Common Faith*, 79.

45. Dewey wrote: "I have been accused more than once and from opposed quarters of an undue, a utopian faith in the possibilities of intelligence and in education as a correlate of intelligence. At all events, I did not invent this faith. I acquired it from my surroundings as far as those surroundings were animated by the democratic spirit. For what is the faith of democracy in the method of consultation, of conference, of persuasion, of discussion, in forming of public opinion, which in the long run is self-corrective, except faith in the capacity of the intelligence of the common man to respond with common sense to the free play of facts and ideas which are secured by effective guarantees of free inquiry, free assembly and free communication? I am willing to leave to upholders of totalitarian states of the right and the left the view that faith in the capacities of intelligence is utopia. For the faith is so deeply embedded in the methods which are intrinsic to democracy that when a professed democrat denies the faith he convicts himself of treachery to his profession." John Dewey, "Creative Democracy," 14–15.

46. "As the values are dwelt upon and carried forward in action they grow in definiteness and coherence. Interaction between aim and existent conditions improves and tests the ideal; and conditions are at the same time modified. Ideals change as they are applied in existent conditions. The process endures and advances with the life of humanity. What one person and one group accomplish becomes the standing ground and starting point of those who succeed them." Dewey, *Common Faith*, 50.

47. Dewey explained: "The war has shown ... that it takes detailed intelligence, not mere desire ... to manage society in an emergency. It has thereby cleared the way for a science of ideas in action which will trust not to negative forces, to bankruptcy, to bring about what is desired, but to positive energy, to intellectual competency, to competency of inquiry, discussion, reflection and invention organized to take effect in action in directing affairs. The result will not be sudden and millennial. But it will be steady; and, as in all experimental science, a mistake will be a source of enlightenment and not a cause of reaction." John Dewey, "A New Social Science" *New Republic* 14 (1918): 294.

48. "No government by experts in which the masses do not have the chance to inform the experts as to their needs can be anything but an oligarchy managed by the interests of the few. And the enlightenment must proceed in ways which force the administrative specialists to take account of the needs. The world has suffered more from leaders and authorities than from the masses." Dewey, *The Public and Its Problems*, 208.

49. Dewey, *The Public and Its Problems*, 211, 208.

50. John Dewey, "Education as Politics," *New Republic* (October 4, 1922): 140, 141.

51. When art classes, school field trips, and the like came under attack in the thirties, Dewey posed the following question concisely: "Do we want to build up and strengthen a class division by means of schools for the masses that confine educa-

tion to a few simple and mechanical skills, while the well-to-do send their children to schools where they get exactly the things that are branded as frills when they are given at public expense to the children of the masses?" Dewey, "Shall We Abolish School 'Frills'? No," *Rotarian* 42 (May 1933): 49.

52. Dewey, *Art as Experience*, 35.

Index